Disclaimer: *Although this book is based on actual experiences of the author, names, dates, titles, and sequences of events have been changed in certain situations to protect the identities of individuals, and dialogue has been paraphrased or simplified. This publication is designed to educate and provide general information regarding the subject matter covered. The author and publisher specifically disclaim any liability resulting from the use or application of the information and material contained in this book, and the information is not intended to serve as legal advice to address individual situations.*

Published by Alouette Enterprises, Inc.

2022 Donna Fridrych

All rights reserved.

No part of this publication may be reproduced, stored in a retrieval system, or transmitted in any form by any means, electronic, mechanical, photocopying, recording, or otherwise, without written permission.

Edited by Carol Gaskin
Cover and design by Debbie Huntsman.
Photograph of the author by Shelley Wolfe Franklin

ISBN — 978-0-9799922-1-6

*To my father
and all the wonderful men
who supported me
throughout my career.*

CONTENTS

Introduction 9

1—Earning Entry into the Business World 13

2—Blatant Discrimination 22

3—Sexual Harassment. 32

4—Intimidation 38

5—Responsibility Without the Title, Pay, or Promotion 50

6—Support and Lack of Support (or Worse) 62

7—A Choice: Act Tough or Be Viewed as Weak 79

8—Using Sexual Appeal in the Workplace 89

9—The Unique Challenge of Meetings. 96

10—Recognition 104

11—Smacking Up Against the Glass Ceiling 111

12 —Compensation Disparity 121

13—The New Millennium—Still Second-in-Command. 130

14—Understanding Negative Perceptions 141

15—Losing a Job. 147

16—Becoming CEO 154

17—Looking Back 161

18—Discrimination Still Exists. 166

19—Yourself: The Final Barrier. 171

CONTENTS

20—Women Are Destined to Excel 182

Steps for Pursuing a Successful Business Career 189

Some Lessons Learned. 192

Questions to Consider. 204

References. 215

About the Author 218

Other Books by Donna Fridrych 219

Introduction

My journey to become acting Chief Information Officer of United Airlines, and then CEO of the United Airlines Employees' Credit Union, was not an easy one. Most women, no matter how successful they have been, have faced most of the same discriminatory experiences I describe in this book. Now, as I write, the Covid-19 pandemic has pushed many women to the brink of exhaustion, caused record numbers to quit their jobs and countless others to question whether they want to continue their careers. Women have had to spend more time juggling work and family life, on top of being marginalized, paid unfairly, ignored in meetings, and sometimes sexually harassed in the workplace. Who wouldn't feel overwhelmed?

Though white women experience many forms of discrimination in the workplace, women of color experience discrimination to a much larger degree. As an example, "Across all racial and ethnic groups, women in the United States are typically paid 83 cents for every dollar paid to men."[1] Women of color, however, especially Latina and Black women, earn about the same as white women did fifty years ago—typically 57 cents for Latinas compared to white, non-Hispanic men, and 64 cents for Black women. While this disparity is partially attributable to pay differences between white-collar and blue-collar jobs, many women from all ethnic backgrounds may understandably believe that discrimination will never get better in their lifetime, and they'll never be able to comfortably balance work and family. They feel beaten down and burned out.

While I fully understand these sentiments, I believe we have reached a tipping point where educated, hardworking, capable women at every level in the workplace will be supported in ways rarely seen in the past. This is not some Pollyannaish, wishful thinking on my part. I believe that we are at a pivotal point in our history, where the onus will be on businesses to make it easier for women to succeed. Contrary to what one might expect, evidence suggests many women are actually gaining traction in their careers.

- According to data from the 2021 Women in the Workplace annual report by McKinsey & Co. and LeanIn.Org.: "For all the change brought on by the pandemic, women in white-collar roles still made strides at nearly every level of U.S. companies ... and the number of women holding some senior roles rose."[2]

- As of June 2021, 41 women were CEOs of Fortune 500 companies in the U.S.[3] While that is just 8%, it is an improvement over many years of stagnation at 5%.

- Recently, multiple studies have concluded that companies with more women at the top fare better in terms of overall effectiveness—including financial strength, customer satisfaction, and innovation.[4]

As women have developed their logical and analytical skills through education and experience, they have also brought their intuitive, holistic, and collaborative gifts into the workplace. This use of balanced skills is the reason women improve a company's bottom line, and why companies are now incentivized to help women flourish by adopting all kinds of innovative programs to support them at work and at home. It is time for women to not only think about what she can do for her company, but to ask what her company can do for her. If a country is wise, it will also help women to succeed, because it needs women in the workforce for its economy to be fully productive.

Despite the support that women may receive from their companies in the future, they will continue to face discrimination, because men do not want to give up their power. While I enjoyed working with men, I also found many who harbored outdated beliefs about women being less capable than men. To help women address these challenges, I describe how I handled specific forms of discrimination in the past, and more importantly, what I would do differently today. I learned that it is important to do something when faced with a discriminatory experience—to in some way acknowledge that the abuse is happening. Doing nothing ... except feeling wronged and angry ... ensures discrimination will continue.

As I tell my story, I resist the temptation to blame all my struggles on men. Instead, I focus on the feelings that discrimination engendered in me: anger (sometimes rage), unworthiness, lack of confidence, and fear of success. These feelings are the internal demons that many women share and need to heal, especially if we want to stop feeling like a victim of the patriarchy. By suggesting ways of handling discrimination, along with addressing these internal emotions, I want to help women shift from feeling disenfranchised to feeling powerful ... from feeling beaten down to enjoying their work.

I conclude the book with several tools to assist women in their career aspirations: a roadmap for pursuing a successful career; a list of some of the lessons I learned throughout my career; and some questions to consider individually or in group discussions.

Most important, I tell women to:
- pursue your dreams;
- feel confident in your choices and abilities; and
- choose again if you are not happy or think you are being treated unfairly.

Wishing you every happiness and success,

Donna

ONE

Earning Entry into the Business World

The year was 1967, my senior year in college. With great excitement and anticipation, a girlfriend and I boarded a train for a trip to the big city—Chicago, where we planned to meet with a recruitment firm. Dressed in a navy-blue skirt and matching vest, an off-white polyester blouse with a loose bow tied around my neck, sixteen hours of calculus under my belt, and dreams of an exciting career, I thought I was a perfect candidate for a business career. Who wouldn't want to hire an attractive, independent, hardworking young woman, someone who had always earned top grades, spent her junior year abroad in Paris, and was soon to graduate with degrees in French and mathematics? Like so many young people from a relatively privileged background, I felt confident that the world was waiting for me to contribute and that I would be successful at whatever I did.

As we sped by cornfields, grazing cows, and small towns in Wisconsin, I gazed out the window and thought about my college years. I didn't have a career counselor back in those days, unless if by some stretch of the imagination you could call my father's well-intentioned but controlling methods counseling. He had insisted he would pay for my college tuition and expenses only if I obtained a math degree and a teaching certificate. With those credentials, he said I would always be able to feed myself and put a roof over my head. My appeals to him to let me study drama and dance fell on deaf ears. In hindsight, my father's insistence on a math degree served me well, as it was a sign to future employers that I was capable of logical thinking.

The university I attended in the States, Marquette University in Milwaukee, Wisconsin, had no stand-alone department of mathematics. Therefore, I had to take all of my classes during my freshman, sophomore, and senior years (even my basic Liberal Arts classes) at the university's engineering school. As a result I was usually one of only a few females in class, and in some cases the only female. Although I found this disconcerting at the time, especially since I had attended an all girls' high school, I learned how to survive and compete in a male-dominated environment, surpassing most of the men in my classes scholastically and tutoring some of the less smart ones.

Fortunately, I thoroughly enjoyed my math classes. I loved the black and white, right or wrong rigor of mathematics; advanced calculus and differential equations challenged my logic-oriented side. I was able to fulfill my creative desires through other means: I choreographed dance routines for musical shows at my university, twirled a baton in parades, joined an ROTC marching unit, and was a cheerleader at some of the Army versus Navy games. And during my wonderful year in Paris, I fell in love, studied literature, and went to the Impressionist museums next to the Tuileries Gardens every week. By the end of my junior year, I had earned half of a master's degree in French. It was hard to come back to the States and finish my math degree.

During my senior year I decided to find a career in business. It sounded much more exciting to me than teaching school. Although I had no idea what kind of jobs I would be eligible for with my background, I strongly believed that a good position would be available for someone with my education.

○ ○ ○ ○

When my girlfriend and I arrived at the recruitment office, the two of us were ushered into a large conference room. Soon, a short, elderly man with a stern-looking face entered and sat down across the table from us. He grunted occasionally, as he quickly scanned the resumes we had given him.

"Girls," he said, looking up, "you have two options. You can be a secretary, or you can be a teacher."

"But I'm not good at typing," I protested, taken aback by his abrupt, dismissive manner. All my attempts in high school to practice my typing skills had failed dismally. Perhaps at a subconscious level, I hadn't wanted to learn how to type because I feared ending up with a secretarial job, so I never improved my skills in speed and accuracy.

"Furthermore, I know I don't want a teaching career," I told the recruiter.

"It's up to you, but there are no other jobs for you." He stood, concluding the five-minute interview, and walked out of the room before my girlfriend even had time to question him.

I sat there in disbelief. I had never once considered I couldn't do anything I put my mind to and worked hard at. I found the prospect of being pigeonholed into what I considered to be predominantly female jobs abhorrent.

Growing up, I had always enjoyed many of the things boys typically did for fun as much as I liked ballet and dancing. When I was seven years old, Dad taught me how to shoot a rifle, which literally knocked me over the first time I pulled the trigger. Later, after I learned how to handle the gun, he took me skeet shooting, which was fun. He encouraged me to do chores that boys often performed, such as mowing the lawn and raking leaves, because he knew I liked to be outside. My father always asked me, and not my brother or mother, to help him with his business plans for the many entrepreneurial businesses he started every few years. When it came to sports, I often beat my brother and his friends when we practiced shooting basketballs in front of our house, and I loved playing tennis. So I could hold my own with the boys. I was not raised to expect a gender bias in anything, and I wasn't intimidated about going into the business arena where I would be competing with men.

But after making more calls to recruitment firms and receiving no encouragement, I reluctantly accepted a teaching job after graduating from college.

Perhaps this was my first mistake ... I succumbed; I abandoned my desires. If I were starting all over today, I would have kept knocking on doors, no matter how many times they were slammed in my face. At least, I hope I would have done so, even if it meant continuing to live with my parents.

Fortunately, for me, the abandonment of my dreams was temporary, although everywhere I looked I saw a male-dominated society. Like so many women and men, the need to put food on my table and a roof over my head forced me to be practical. But what I shouldn't have done is give up my dream of having a successful business career. I have learned to never, ever give up on my dreams.

○ ○ ○ ○

Those few years of teaching French and math after graduating from college were frustrating for me. My heart was not into teaching, which only made me feel guilty for not loving the profession, as so many of my fellow teachers seemed to do. Although I worked hard and became head of the French department for my school district, I was depressed about not being able to work at something I loved. Furthermore, I had decided I didn't want to get married until I had established a successful career (and in my mind, that didn't include teaching school). I feared a man would try to control me and tell me what to do, as my father had done so much of the time with my mother and me.

I began to have panic attacks. My first dreadful experience happened when I was walking on a crowded street in downtown Chicago and began to feel dizzy; I looked up to see several tall buildings swaying back and forth ... like flags in the wind. My heart began racing. From that day forward, a panic attack could descend on me anytime and anywhere with a variety of symptoms. Usually my symptoms included sweaty palms, distorted eyesight, a racing heart, and an overwhelming sense of urgency to flee wherever I was. I often feared I would die during the attack.

Unfortunately, panic attacks had not been identified as an illness at the time, and therefore the psychiatrist I consulted did not have good advice for me. He didn't even have a name for what I was experiencing, which made me feel even more fearful. I felt terribly ashamed and didn't want anyone to know what was happening to me, especially since I thought most people saw me as a strong, independent woman.

Fortunately, I had an exceptionally strong will—a will that refused to allow panic attacks to run my life. Also, I was fortunate to have a sensitive, compassionate mother—someone I could talk to about my fears and whom I could count on to support me. As painful as most situations were for me at the time, I felt safest when I was teaching. In that way, becoming a teacher was a godsend.

Another thing that helped me get through the panic attacks was learning how to knit from Maryla, one of the older teachers at my school. Knitting allowed me to focus on the rhythm of the needles as I worked a pattern; it became a form of meditation. Knitting would become a hobby that helped me through many stressful times in my life, resulting in afghans, ponchos, vests, and scarves for myself and my family.

Though there were many reasons for the onslaught of this disease, I believe giving up my dream of having a career in business added to my depression and contributed to my experiencing panic attacks. While I fought back against my debilitating emotions and did not consider suicide, I can understand how giving up one's dreams and desires could lead to such an outcome, especially for young people.

Eventually my panic attacks diminished in intensity and frequency. I believed overcoming them had made me a stronger person. Later in my life, this newfound strength would help me to carry out difficult business decisions and survive personal hardships. What I had considered the worst thing that had ever happened to me taught me that there is always some shred of positivity—a silver lining—in all of life's events, even the most difficult ones.

In addition, I was later able to help a young man and a young woman through their unexpected episodes; the woman, whom I had never met, had a full-blown panic attack while sitting next to me on an airplane. As she screamed and her eyes bulged in fright, I held her hands tightly and tried to calm her, especially during takeoff and landing, when she seemed certain we would crash. The young man was one of my employees, whose shame I was able to lessen through our discussions.

Experiencing panic attacks humbled me. Previously, I considered myself a brave, smart, confident, invincible woman, one who had fearlessly traveled all over Europe by herself. After experiencing panic attacks, I developed empathy for other people's struggles ... especially those with an emotional or psychological disorder.

∘ ∘ ∘ ∘

After my first year as a teacher, I decided to interview to be a Kelly Girl during the summer months, partly to relieve my boredom but mainly to earn extra money. Kelly Girl jobs were usually temporary secretarial assignments. Although I didn't want to be a secretary, I thought it would at least give me a chance to be in the business world. Day after day in the Kelly Girl office, I would sit at my typewriter, practicing my typing skills and watching with frustration as other women were placed at client sites. My typing skills were so bad that the agency couldn't place me anywhere—I typed too slowly to meet the agency's criteria for job placement, and I made too many mistakes if I increased my typing speed. As I mentioned earlier, I'm sure I had some kind of mental block against typing, because there was nothing wrong with my brain and hand-eye coordination; I had even enjoyed playing lively tunes on the piano as a young girl.

There was one other job, after my sophomore year in college, at which I had also been a dismal failure: working as a waitress at a high-end restaurant called The Top of the Rock in Milwaukee, Wisconsin. In spite of all the training that the new waitresses received, one other girl and I were never allowed to wait on a table by ourselves; we were required to always work together as a team. The two of us would laugh hysterically when one of us would accidentally spill ice cubes out of the pitcher onto the table, or drop salad leaves onto the floor while tossing the salad. Once, I even dropped a tray-load of steaks in the lap of a young man wearing a tux who had come to the restaurant after his homecoming dance. I didn't laugh about that. It was hard to believe I wasn't fired on the spot. I often wondered how someone with all my dance experience could be so clumsy.

Finally, after several weeks of sitting in the Kelly Girl office, I was placed in a job at the American Library Association in downtown Chicago. The manager at the association had been told that I couldn't type very fast, so he tailored a job for me. The work consisted of typing book titles and other basic information on index cards and then filing them in a file cabinet—a job that did not require fast typing.

○ ○ ○ ○

During my second summer after teaching school, I was hired to be one of the first female bartenders at a well-known bar and eatery in Chicago—Butch McGuire's, a popular hangout for locals and visitors. I knew I hadn't been hired because of the math and French degrees on my resume; I think telling them during my interview that I had been homecoming queen for an all-boys school during my senior year in high school was more important to them.

On my first day on the job, I wore a pair of navy-blue cotton slacks; the supervisor took me aside and told me I needed to wear shorts. On my second day on the job, I came in wearing shorts, and my supervisor told me I needed to wear shorter shorts. I thought my shorts were short enough, so I didn't comply with his request, and I wasn't fired.

For the most part, I enjoyed talking to the mostly male customers who sat at the bar. One time, when a customer became a little too forward and fresh, I simply tipped over a glassful of beer onto his lap. Then I threw my hands over my mouth and exclaimed how sorry I was to have caused the accident. Fortunately, I didn't have to do that very often.

During that summer I found a book at my local bookstore that would change my life—a book that I regrettably lost in one of my house moves. I no longer remember the title, but it was a self-help book similar to the later, popular *What Color Is Your Parachute?*[5]—a guide for helping people choose suitable careers. Through the use of a series of questions and situational testing, the book encouraged me to believe that a career in computers would be a perfect fit for me.

I knew nothing about computers. They had never been mentioned in my classes at Marquette and were not widely used in business in the sixties. So I enrolled in a class to learn about computer hardware at a YMCA in downtown Chicago.

Computers at that time were massive, taking up most of the space in a large room. After that class I bought several books about software and worked diligently to teach myself three computer languages: Assembler (a low-level programming language consisting mostly of symbolic equivalents); COBOL (one of the earliest high-level business-oriented languages); and FORTRAN (a high-level programming language that was sometimes used for formula and scientific-oriented programming).

Feeling confident, after several years of self-study, that I had a good grasp of both computer hardware and software, I sent one hundred resumes to various large companies. In spite of my dad telling me not to mention my bartending experience on my resume, I did so anyway. I didn't want anyone to think I was just some kind of computer nerd.

I was overwhelmed by the response. Big companies like IBM and Allstate Insurance asked to interview me. What I didn't know until years later was that companies were being required at that time to hire minorities in order to obtain certain contracts, particularly government contracts.

After deliberating over several job offers, I accepted a job with one of the Big Eight accounting firms, Arthur Andersen & Co., which had a burgeoning computer consulting division. My decision was largely based on the extensive training the firm would initially provide me to become a consultant. I couldn't wait to begin my new career.

As I look back, my father's insistence on my getting a math degree, and my own initiative to study and learn computer languages, were key determinants of how my life would progress. My panic attacks all but disappeared as I focused on my new, exciting career. I found it remarkable how quickly I healed myself of those dreadful experiences. All it had taken was the renewal of my hopes and dreams.

TWO

Blatant Discrimination

When I started my new job at the accounting firm, I soon realized that I was one of the first women hired into their consulting division; only three other women in a group of hundreds of men had been hired at about the same time. We were all enrolled in a three-month training program at an off-site school.

Our intensive training program was often referred to as "boot camp," because of the long hours and challenging assignments. Everyone was required to live on campus, except for some rare breaks. This added to our feeling pressured, because we felt as though we were always being watched and evaluated. Late-night classes and difficult homework assignments were intended to prepare us for the long, grueling hours ahead of us as consultants.

Some of the men dropped out of the training program after only a few weeks because they couldn't keep up with the assignments; I heard that several of them had suffered nervous breakdowns. I was determined not to be one of the failures.

Three months later, after successfully completing the training program, I was put in charge of my first assignment. The project entailed developing a nurse scheduling system for a hospital. Although I was surprised that I had been placed in a supervisory role right out of training, especially since all seven of the male colleagues I supervised had more business education than me, I assumed I had done better than the men in the training program. Perhaps it was also because I was a few years older than the men; I was twenty-six, and they had all just graduated from college. Rather than trying to find reasons (excuses) for why I had been put in a supervisory role, I should have celebrated the fact and taken the opportunity to boost my self-confidence.

It didn't take long for me to realize that most of my male coworkers, who had joined the firm at the same time I did, had been given a higher title than I had; I assumed they also earned better pay. The fact is that in 1972, when I joined the company, women were paid less than 60% of what men earned for equivalent work—a statistic I was fortunately not aware of at the time. But believe it or not, the lower title and pay didn't bother me too much then. First of all, I figured that most of the men I worked with had earned business degrees, whereas I had a liberal arts degree, and I assumed that my degree was not as valued in the business world. Second, I loved my job and felt confident that if I worked hard, in time I would be rewarded with a better position and pay. I had even taken a pay cut from my teaching position when I joined the accounting firm. Money was not important to me at the time. I just wanted the opportunity to learn as much as I could about computers and consulting. Having three roommates, I was able to live comfortably on twenty dollars a week for food and sundries.

Looking back, by not challenging my lower pay, I set myself up for diminished compensation for my entire career. Again, rather than trying to find reasons (excuses) for my lower pay, I should have at least made inquiries as to why my title and therefore salary was lower than that of my mostly male colleagues.

The partner in charge of my first project rarely stopped in to see us, so that left me relatively free to run the project as I saw fit. The nurse scheduling system was completed on time and within budget and installed at the hospital. I was proud of our success and hoped I would be rewarded … if not now, then later.

Shortly after completing my first project, I was scheduled to attend a celebratory luncheon for my firm at a club that was only a few blocks from one of our offices in downtown Chicago. So I and two of my colleagues, Brad and John, decided to walk there. As I was walking down the sidewalk between the two men, they suddenly turned down an alleyway.

"Where are we going?" I asked, as I continued walking with them. I was surprised that we had turned off the sidewalk of the busy downtown area and couldn't help but worry that my new, white high-heeled shoes would be ruined by walking on the black cinders in the alley.

Neither of the young men answered my question. I focused on placing my feet as gingerly as possible into the cinders to avoid ruining my shoes. We walked about a half a block down the alley, until we were facing the rear of a brick, soot-covered building with several large doors and a turnstile entrance. Brad and John stepped aside and motioned for me to enter the turnstile first.

Inside, the room in front of me looked like a basement or a delivery area. "Why are we going in here?" I asked my colleagues, and then a Black bellman appeared, fully arrayed in a formal uniform and wearing white gloves.

"Why, don't you know, ma'am?" the bellman replied pleasantly. "Women aren't allowed through the front entrance of the club."

"What!" I shouted in disbelief and abruptly stopped walking, as Brad and John, looking somewhat frightened, came through the turnstile to join me. "You can't be serious."

I could hardly believe what the bellman had said. This was the seventies. Yet I knew the bellman must be telling the truth; otherwise, why would my two colleagues have escorted me down the alley and be looking so sheepish now?

After recovering from my shock, I knew I had a decision to make. Would I attend the luncheon, or would I boycott the event?

I tried to calm my turbulent emotions and swallow my anger as we followed the bellman to an elevator. No one talked as we rode the elevator to the second-floor restaurant. I was so upset at the time that I was barely able to think, let alone talk.

When the elevator doors opened, the bellman escorted us to a reception desk. After giving the hostess my name, I was seated at a luncheon table with seven men. I remember distinctly, as if it was yesterday, how I sat meekly at a table, eating very little and hardly speaking. More than anything, I was trying not to cry.

Although I had already fought many battles by my young age of twenty-seven, this seemed to be the most humiliating experience I had encountered thus far. I couldn't help but reflect on how African Americans must feel, having been subjected to similar discriminatory treatment for more than a century.

How could a major company provide business to a club like that in the seventies? I asked myself. And even if I gave the club every benefit of the doubt, concluding that it was trying to protect men's privacy because it primarily served as an athletic club—though we were eating in the club's restaurant, not in the gym—the point was that I never seemed to fit into the social venues. Exceptions had to be made to accommodate my presence on too many occasions.

I went home that night feeling depressed, thinking that all my years of working hard, striving to do my best in school, and fighting my way into the business world were for naught. I feared I would always be an outsider to the men who controlled the business world and that I would never be considered an equal. And I couldn't help wondering, if women weren't viewed as equal to men, then how hard was it going to be for me to be successful in the business world?

∘ ∘ ∘ ∘

The day after the luncheon, I was scheduled to spend some time in our corporate office instead of at my client's site. Actually, I would have preferred to be at my client's office, because they would not have known about my humiliation of the previous day.

After checking my mail, I walked to the open office area reserved for consultants who were spending the day in the office. Perhaps it was only my imagination, but I felt as if some of my colleagues were avoiding eye contact with me. I sat down at a table next to Brad.

"Are we playing tennis tomorrow night?" I asked him, trying to act as if nothing unusual had happened the previous day. I played tennis weekly with three of my male colleagues whenever I was in town.

"I'm planning on it. About yesterday ... I know that was a shock to you. I'm sorry it happened."

"When did you find out you were going to have to escort me to the back entrance?"

"Not until right before John and I left the office yesterday. We were pretty upset, as I'm sure you were. John and I had only a few minutes to talk about what to do, before you walked up to us. We didn't know if we should have refused to escort you. What would you have wanted us to do?"

"I don't know. I guess I would have preferred if you had first walked with me to the front entrance. Then if we had been refused entry, which probably would have happened, I would have liked to see the three of us turn around and leave without attending the luncheon. Of course, hindsight is always easy. I also feel that I shouldn't have gone into the luncheon once I found out the reason we had to use the back entrance."

"There's nothing we can do about yesterday," Brad said, "but John and I talked last night about what we should do now. At a minimum, we are going to write a note to the head of the firm and get as many signatures as we can. At least we can try to prevent this from happening again. We will suggest that if the club doesn't change its rules and allow women to enter through the front door, then our firm should disassociate itself from the establishment."

"I hope you don't get into trouble over this."

"If we do, then I'm not sure this is the place for me to work. I talked to my sister last night about how she might feel if the same thing had happened to her. She was shocked and said she probably would have started cursing or crying."

Although I was grateful that Brad and John were upset on my behalf and took action to change how I had been treated, I think this was the beginning of my internalizing my anger … or at least not addressing my anger. I did nothing about the injustice. I meekly acquiesced and tried to pretend the humiliation hadn't occurred. By letting others fight my battles—especially when those others were men—I felt weak and disempowered. I hadn't learned how to stand up for myself and fight my own battles. I wished I had not gone into the luncheon and had marched right into the Human Resources (HR) department to file a complaint.

Prior to this event, I had usually expressed my anger at unjust treatment. When I was child, I either cried or yelled at my father for his heavy-handed treatment of my mother or me. I commiserated with the few other women in my division about our lower titles and pay, but I had grown tired of hearing my few female coworkers complain. I didn't want to complain all the time and sound like they did. This was probably an unwise decision for me because suppressed anger would be a demon I battled my entire life.

○ ○ ○ ○

In addition to Brad and John, several other men in the firm went out of their way to help me. One of them was Michael, a senior partner in the firm. Michael did not fit the mold of most of the other partners. His dress was not as polished, and his face was often slightly unshaven. But most important, he treated me with respect and always seemed concerned as to how I was feeling. Without saying anything to me directly, I got the feeling that he knew it was difficult for me to be one of the few women among thousands of men.

Early on in my career, I had decided that I would not try to hide my femininity by dressing in a mannish way or cutting my hair short. I often wore the stylish wrap-around dresses that Diane von Furstenberg made popular in the seventies. I wore makeup and set my long, blonde hair in rollers every night. In other words, I didn't feel it should be necessary for me to compromise my fashion style to fit into the boys' club and be respected for my mind.

One day Michael set up an appointment to meet with me. As I sat down in his office, I felt somewhat nervous, because I didn't know what to expect.

"How would you like to develop a course to teach basic accounting and financial reporting to some high-level executives?" he asked me, after we had exchanged the usual pleasantries. "We have quite a few clients who have somehow made it to the top of their companies without learning some of the basic principles of accounting and finance. With your teaching background, I thought you would know how to develop such a course."

"I'd love to do that," I said.

After Michael gave me some further direction, I developed the course. Then he asked me to teach the course a few months later.

As I stood in front of a group of eight CEOs, teaching them the basics of financial reporting and accounting, I felt proud and competent. I may have had only a junior consultant title, but I felt knowledgeable well beyond my pay grade. It was also the first time that I realized how ill-equipped these senior men were to handle their jobs. I wondered how they could have reached their positions without basic understanding of finance and reporting.

○ ○ ○ ○

One day, I was at our corporate office when Brad was there again as well.

"Did you get your invitation for the summer outing?" he asked me. "I hope you're planning on playing tennis with us."

"No, I haven't gotten it yet. I checked my mail this morning."

"You should have gotten it by now. Why don't you ask the secretary on duty if she has it?"

I honestly didn't imagine there was any problem, but I went to talk to a secretary as Brad had suggested.

"One of the partners told me that you are more than welcome to attend the dinner," the secretary said, after following up on my inquiry.

"What about playing tennis?"

"He specifically said you could attend the dinner only. The tennis and golf event is just for the men."

"I can understand that the partners might think women aren't good at these sports, but I've been playing tennis most of my life. In fact, I play weekly with three guys in the firm. Would you please tell him that?"

"I can talk to him again, but I assure you he was very definitive about it when he told me that you weren't supposed to play tennis. Wives are also being invited only to the dinner."

"Well, I'm not a wife. I am a consultant in this firm," I said indignantly, even though I knew the secretary was only relating what she had been told.

I was left with several choices, none of which was appealing to me. I could decline the invitation to the event; I could try to convince the partners to let me play tennis; or I could just attend the dinner. After much deliberation, I decided to attend the dinner and not make an issue about playing tennis. I reasoned that the dinner was almost a command performance, as well as a good opportunity to socialize with the partners in the firm. If I had chosen to make an issue about not being able to play tennis, the conflict may have drawn negative attention to me and possibly cast me in an unfavorable light.

○ ○ ○ ○

I did not enjoy the evening at the summer outing. I felt I had let myself down, even though I knew that if I had decided to fight this battle and been able to play tennis, I probably would not have enjoyed the game; I would have felt unduly pressured to play well. I had already reached the point in my career where I was selective about which battles I chose to fight.

By now, I was frequently angry about the inequality of my title and my pay, in addition to being upset about incidents like the summer outing. I knew that I was being paid less than many of my male colleagues who were doing the same work, because I still had a lower title than most of them. There were also men who openly bragged about their salary.

I knew that the anger I was feeling was not healthy for me. But as the months went by and I wasn't promoted, I became even angrier. The few other women in my division shared my complaint—that although we were given significant responsibility for our rank, we were not given due credit in terms of pay and promotions for our accomplishments. Moreover, we didn't seem to be on the fast-track career path like many of our male counterparts.

My performance evaluations were always glowing, which further added to my anger over not being promoted. The only room for improvement ever noted was that I needed to exude more confidence. I wondered if that meant strutting around and crowing like a proud rooster, which I saw many of the top men do; I would never have been comfortable doing that, although I did think my inner self-confidence needed a boost. I often felt beaten down by the exclusion I felt and the little battles I had to fight day after day.

I was afraid to ask for a promotion. I didn't want to appear ungrateful for being given the opportunity to be a consultant, and I feared I might lose my job if I made too many demands. I just hoped someone would notice the unfairness of my title and pay, and promote me.

As Sheryl Sandberg, Chief Operating Officer for Facebook, explains in a *Wall Street Journal* (*WSJ*) article, "Women who negotiate are 67% more likely than women who don't to receive feedback that their personal style is 'intimidating,' 'too aggressive,' or 'bossy,' and they are more likely to receive that kind of feedback than men who negotiate."[6]

It's hard for me to look back and think about how I took no action to stand up for myself, mostly because I was afraid of the consequences.

I loved the work I was doing and the challenges provided by my assignments. I enjoyed working with men and the analytical thinking that computer programming required, while pitying the women who were subjected to secretarial and inconsequential duties. I didn't want to become like them. Therefore, I shut my mouth over injustices done to me and did not challenge the system. Although the extensive travel required for my job was tiring, I performed my duties without complaint, diligently working the ten- to twelve-hour days that were expected of junior consultants like me.

Perhaps most important is that I did not take credit for my accomplishments. I did not take credit for being the supervisor on my first assignment over men who had more education than me; I did not take credit for frequently being given the hardest computer programs on engagements; I didn't acknowledge that my skills in many ways were superior to those of the CEOs to whom I taught a refresher course. Rather, I let the system—the lower title and pay—erode my fragile self-confidence.

Given all the negative signs, I now understand how I allowed my confidence to diminish. It's hard to feel good about yourself when you are being treated in an unfair, dismissive manner, while trying to keep your job and get ahead. But it is so important to not let others belittle your accomplishments or damage your self-esteem. True, a wage gap today of 17% for white women is not as bad as the 40% gap that I experienced, but remains unfair. It's also true that women of color are still experiencing a similar wage gap to what I experienced. There are many avenues for women to raise issues of unfairness, but I would say the most important thing is to not let your self-esteem be eroded ... no matter what.

THREE

Sexual Harassment

Sexual harassment seemed to be an important topic in most companies where I worked, especially as more women moved into management careers. In one company, all the managers and supervisors were required to attend sexual harassment training on what was called the "zero-tolerance" policy; in other words, no sexual harassment of any kind was to be tolerated.

In theory, I supported the notion that no woman should be made to feel threatened or uncomfortable with sexual innuendos or actions, but I felt too much ado was being made over the issue. I believed that sexually explicit comments should not be tolerated, but that reading harassment into comments intended as harmless could be counterproductive. But in retrospect I was, without a doubt, too dismissive in my beliefs.

Although I was frequently upset about discrimination in terms of promotions and pay, I was rarely upset for long about sexual harassment. This is probably because, aside from some references to my attractiveness or the occasional off-color joke being told while in a group, I never considered myself to have been sexually harassed at work.

Sexual harassment is defined as "unwelcome sexual advances, requests for sexual favors, and other verbal or physical conduct of a sexual nature that tends to create a hostile or offensive work environment."[7] Given that definition, there were certainly instances at work that I could have claimed as sexual harassment, as most women could as well. How many women haven't been in a group of men where the discussion or jokes have been of a sexual nature?

On the occasions when I did chafe at sexual comments, perhaps I should have realized that my feelings of discomfort were creating or adding to my less confident and less powerful frame of mind than my male colleagues.

○ ○ ○ ○

While working on an engagement that was not going well for the firm, I was asked to pitch in and help do some computer programming at the client's site. The head client was the Chief Information Officer (CIO) of a Fortune 100 company to whom I and some of my colleagues had been briefly introduced when we joined the project.

One afternoon I was sitting at my desk in a large room with seven other consultants, reviewing the code of my computer program. Footsteps on the tile floor disrupted the silence in the room, and I looked up to see the project manager from my firm. He was walking toward my desk. I was surprised to see him, because he usually didn't bother to talk to any of us programmers. Then he sat down in the chair next to my desk.

"How's your program coming along?" he asked me, in a casual-sounding voice.

"Pretty well. I should be finished by the end of next week," I said, smelling the tantalizing aroma from the popcorn bag he held in his hand.

"That's good news," he said, as he slowly opened the bag of popcorn. "You know, the CIO is not happy about our progress on this project. You've met him, haven't you?"

"Only once ... with a group of other people."

"Well, I'm sure he remembers you, given how attractive you are."

I didn't respond. I felt uncomfortable with his comment. Brad was sitting at the desk in front of me, just a few feet away. I wondered if he was listening.

"Why don't you take this popcorn and offer some to the CIO?" he asked, as he moved the bag of popcorn toward me in his outstretched hand. "You might sit down and talk to him for a while. I know he's in his office now, and he's free."

"I'd feel stupid," I said, not taking the popcorn bag from him and feeling my face blush. "I'm really not comfortable doing that. Perhaps someone else should do it."

He stood up, gave me a perturbed frown, and walked away without saying anything else.

Brad turned around and rolled his eyes at me, shaking his head from side to side. Obviously, he had overheard the conversation.

I felt embarrassed that my manager would ask me to do something as demeaning as trying to flirt with the client. And underneath my embarrassment was anger. How dare he put me in a position of doing something so ludicrous or risk disobeying the boss?

This may seem like a small incident, but my feelings of humiliation and embarrassment were intense. For a brief moment, I thought about talking to the National Organization for Women (NOW), whose representatives had contacted me on several occasions. Although I believed such organizations were important, I didn't want to be affiliated with any kind of militant action or boycotting. I was also afraid of the consequences if my firm were to discover I was participating in the organization. The NOW group had picketed in front of my firm's corporate offices, and I was grateful that I had been at a client site on the day of that protest.

Instead, that night I called my friend Cary, who was fighting her own battles at the company where she worked as the only female realtor. Cary told me that on several occasions when she had returned to her office, the papers she had left on her desk were scattered around the room, missing, or thrown into various wastebaskets; she had solved the problem by making sure to lock all of her papers inside her desk before leaving her office. She didn't know who was responsible for the vandalism, but she doubted that the men in the office ever experienced the same kind of problem. Cary also told me that many of the men made it known that they didn't appreciate having a woman take the place that a man could fill in the realty company. Although circumstances would change over the next decades, this fundamental issue of women taking positions away from men would continue to be a source of angst for some men.

"I understand how you feel," Cary responded, after I had told her what had happened that afternoon. "It sounds as if it's a reasonable request on the surface. We understand the innuendo, but he didn't actually tell you outright to flirt with the CIO or anything."

"I know, but he made me feel so foolish. I can't imagine myself walking into the CIO's office and offering him popcorn. I'm just a lowly programmer here. You know, I must admit, I work hard at looking sexy and attractive. That's how I grew up—always trying to look my best and appear eye-catching for men. But I thought at some point I would be valued more for my intellect and job performance."

"Sometimes I don't think that's ever going to happen. I think some men can't handle their sexual fantasies about us, and they just try harder to put us in our place."

After my discussion with Cary, I decided once again to ignore what had happened and hope my manager on my next job would be more respectful. But each time I backed down and chose not to make an issue over these humiliating incidents, I lost a little bit more of my soul and became a lot angrier. Although I did not realize it at the time, my frustration and anger were affecting me physically; I experienced frequent stomachaches, and talking to my girlfriends who were fighting similar battles only seemed to get me more worked up.

○ ○ ○ ○

Although self-help books were becoming popular in the seventies, I was so caught up in my work that I didn't take the time to learn how to productively express my angry feelings. I continued to try to bury my anger.

The popcorn incident, while disturbing and embarrassing, was not something I thought of as sexual harassment. To my mind, sexual harassment was a serious crime, not irritating and stupid adolescent behavior by grown men who should have known better how to act.

Perhaps I had become jaded, because in college and my early working career, I worked almost exclusively with men and became used to not reacting to comments of a sexual nature. Perhaps the instances of physical sexual assault I had experienced outside of the work environment (once by two teenage boys, another time by a gynecologist, and then by a date in my early twenties) lowered my standard for what I considered to be sexual harassment. Those incidents left permanent scars on my psyche, whereas I was able to brush aside the crude remarks and suggestions of male colleagues and bosses.

Sexual harassment is a difficult issue to deal with for many reasons. First, there is the discomfort in calling out someone who has made a sexual comment. No one wants to be seen as prudish, and most people don't want to bring attention to themselves by raising the topic. Then there is the uncomfortable task of having to repeat the comment or action to a supervisor. The main reason, of course, is that many women fear the consequences to their career from filing a sexual harassment suit or complaint; they worry such charges will hinder or halt their career advancement. For this reason many women don't come forward, even when they have been propositioned, until they are fired for other reasons or somehow sidetracked in their careers. All in all, it often seems easier to ignore comments or actions of a sexual nature.

As I mentioned earlier, I had decided it was wise to carefully pick my battles in the workplace. For me, it was equally offensive to be maligned, ignored, or treated in a dismissive fashion professionally as it was to be harassed by sexual verbiage or insinuations. Fair pay and promotions were far more important to me than being concerned about a bunch of immature men standing around telling dirty jokes. So unless someone overtly propositioned me or physically accosted me, I decided to tolerate the occasional dirty joke or sexual innuendo.

Yet if I were in the workforce today, I would take the men to task for making crude remarks of a sexual nature or asking me to flirt with a client. By making it clear that I would not tolerate such conduct, I would be helping myself and other women to not be subjected to such harassment.

Today I recognize that my failure to address even subtle sexual comments hurt my self-esteem. Comments of a sexual nature caused me to feel uncomfortable and disrespected. Sexual comments often make fun of women, or worse yet, denigrate female sexuality—something that should be revered.

Sexual harassment is a topic that I feel much differently about today than I did as a younger woman. Other than calling the American Medical Association (AMA) when I was sexually abused by a gynecologist, I never told anyone about the other, physical sexual abuses I experienced, and I never called out any men for making sexual remarks. Shame and discomfort kept me silent. The AMA never followed up on my horrible experience; I should have called them again. Inaction by me and other women of my era enabled the behavior that the #MeToo movement is addressing now. A half-century later, we are still fighting the same battles.

In the 1970s, as I began to build my career, I was simply not equipped to handle sexual harassment. I sorely regret not learning how to do so and encourage the young women of today to maintain their self-esteem, speak up, and assert their ideas and expertise.

FOUR

Intimidation

Most of my assignments thus far had involved computer programming and design, and lasted for many months. I had also performed computer audits for Commonwealth Edison, a large utility provider in Illinois; for Bell and Howell, a manufacturer of cameras, lenses, and motion picture machinery; and for several smaller banks and financial institutions. I did computer design work and programming for General Electric and was offered an out-of-state job, which I declined because I was working on an MBA at Loyola University in Chicago. I had done programming work at the headquarters of United Airlines and a statistical analysis job for the University of Chicago, in addition to overseeing the implementation of a nurse scheduling system for a hospital in Milwaukee, Wisconsin, mentioned earlier. My latest assignment had been as the lead designer for a computer system at a company that manufactured industrial diamonds in Columbus, Ohio. I can honestly say that I was fascinated by and enjoyed every job.

One of the big differences between me and my few female colleagues at the Big Eight firm was that once an engagement was over, I put all the slights and hurts from the previous job aside and began the new one with a hopeful, positive outlook. Whereas my colleagues in the division continued to complain about their past treatment, I looked forward to my new assignment. This ability to always look on the bright side was a skill I had learned from my mother—a skill that some might consider Pollyannaish, but one I thought served me well.

○ ○ ○ ○

At this point in my story, I have decided to be circumspect and somewhat vague about identifying the companies I worked at for two reasons: First, my intent for writing this book is not to shame specific people; and second, my lawyer has recommended discretion. What I can reveal is that my next assignment for Arthur Anderson & Co. was at a Fortune 500 company that had a reputation for treating women well. Therefore, I was in an upbeat mood going into my next engagement.

I arrived at the Kansas City airport early on a Sunday afternoon and checked into my hotel near the company's headquarters. I wanted to feel fresh and rested the following morning when I would report for my new assignment. Finding my recently renovated hotel room to be much nicer than the ones I usually stayed in buoyed my spirits even more. Although I had received little information about this new job, I had heard it was an important one for my firm.

When I met the partner in charge of the project the next morning, he quickly brushed me aside and turned me over to the person who would be my manager for the duration of the project. I was surprised by the partner's lack of polish and professional grooming. His shirt, his hair, and everything about his appearance was disheveled. The manager to whom I reported, however, looked as if he had just walked out of an advertising catalogue for an MBA program. He was a short, good-looking, clean-shaven young man with a stern demeanor. His manner was stiff and formal as he got right down to business, showing me my desk and explaining my assignment.

The project consisted of redoing all the computer systems for the client company—from manufacturing to marketing to accounting. My assignment was to design and program the inventory control and distribution systems. This was clearly one of the more difficult parts of the project, in part due to the complex nature of the business and the wide variety of company products.

The difficulty of the assignment didn't bother me, but I was disturbed by the proposed schedule. It was April, and the manager said all the systems were scheduled to be finished by July. At first I thought I must have misunderstood either the assignment or the year in which it was to be completed. I knew it would be impossible to complete such a task in that limited timeframe—not unlikely, *impossible*.

"I don't think the end date for this assignment is achievable," I said after he had finished describing my assignment. "I'm sure you know it takes months just to do the design for complex systems like this, let alone complete the programming and all the unit and interface testing with the other systems."

"Well, you'd better figure out a way to do it," he answered, walking away from my cubicle.

What a jerk! I thought, convinced that there was something seriously wrong with this project.

I decided to talk to the client analyst whom my manager had said understood the business requirements. As we talked, I found him to be an intelligent, kind man, and I immediately felt comfortable with him.

"Your firm is the third consulting firm that's been in here over the past ten years," the client analyst said.

"Do you think we're going to be successful?" I asked.

"Are you kidding? You have three months to go, and you don't even have all the programs designed yet."

"What do you think is going to happen?"

"For sure, the systems won't cut over on time. But our company will probably negotiate an extension, just like they always do, and end up paying more money than they should."

"Do your superiors really think the project is going to be done on time?"

"I don't know, but your firm keeps reporting that all the systems are going to cutover in July."

The client had confirmed my assessment of the project and my assignment. I decided to study the business requirements for the rest of the day and think overnight about how I would handle my predicament.

○ ○ ○ ○

The next day I went to my manager's office to talk to him frankly. "I've thought a lot about my assignment since yesterday," I said, sitting down across from him, "and I'm very confident I know how to design the system. I designed a similar one for a company that manufactured industrial diamonds. Although that system was on a smaller scale, the concept is the same. But I must tell you again that I can't come close to meeting your schedule. Last night I laid out my most optimistic estimates, even considering I will work twelve-hour days." I passed him a sheet of paper with a timeline.

"I'm not interested in your estimates or timeline," he said, not even glancing at the information I had prepared. "I gave you your timeline and estimates yesterday."

"But I'm telling you I can't do it. If you think someone else can do it, then you should get him in here. I'm telling you I know for sure I can't do it," I said firmly.

"You have to, and that's the end of the discussion." Then he stood up and walked out of his office.

This is insane! I thought to myself. *I don't get it. Any idiot who knows anything about computer systems would realize this project can't be done in that timeframe. Why won't he listen to me—or find somebody else to do the job who thinks it can be done?*

For the rest of the day, I sat in my cubicle and stewed over what I should do. I found it difficult to concentrate. Perhaps I was just being paranoid, but I couldn't help thinking that some of the clients were looking at me strangely when I walked through the hallways to go to the restroom. I knew I must have looked angry and upset, because I had not learned how to hide my emotions. I wondered if that ability would come later on, after I had gained more experience in the business world.

Late that afternoon, after most of the client personnel had left the office, my manager walked into my cubicle. "Your desk is being moved into the partner's office," he said. "You are not supposed to talk to anyone about your concerns, certainly not to any of the clients. This is our firm's business."

I was speechless. While I knew it was commonplace for a consulting company to put off telling a client that a project was in trouble, I couldn't believe a peon like me was being moved into the partner's office so I would keep my mouth shut. I could have punched my pipsqueak of a manager.

Two men came into my cubicle and lifted my desk and chair onto a cart. I meekly followed them as they rolled the cart to the partner's office. Then I watched from the doorway as they shoved my desk and chair into the small office that was not much larger than an eight by twelve cubicle. The disheveled-looking partner in charge of the project was sitting at his desk, but he didn't even look up from his paperwork.

I walked into the office with my legs shaking from fury, sat down in my chair, and stared at the blank wall in front of me.

After I had spent about an hour looking at the wall or staring at my notebook, the partner packed up his briefcase and left the office without having said a word to me. I had been too upset to work. Although my legs had stopped shaking, I now felt sick to my stomach.

At the time, I couldn't think of anyone who would believe me if I told them what had happened and how I was being intimidated, except for my realtor friend Cary, who had been a victim of intimidation herself. Just thinking about how the partner had tried to coerce me into silence by moving my desk into his office infuriated me. It didn't take long for me to decide that this was definitely a cause to do battle over; I refused to be intimidated.

∘ ∘ ∘ ∘

That night I called a colleague whom I trusted to tell him what had happened, and I asked him if he would deliver a letter that I had written to the head of our firm. I suppose I could have contacted the HR department, but I felt this was more of a business issue than a personnel issue. I also did not have a boss to go to at our home offices; my only boss was the manager I reported to on the engagement—the one who had threatened and dismissed me. I had decided I wasn't going to be part of a conspiracy to grossly lie to the client or be the fall guy for the project. Although I feared I might lose my job, regardless of whether or not I took any action, I felt so angry that I had to do something.

During the next several days, I sat at my desk in the partner's office and focused on my assignment, knowing that it had to be done even if I was replaced on the project. I felt calmer now that I had written and sent the letter. The partner was rarely in his office, but when he occasionally came in, he ignored me, and I kept my head down and continued working. It was a strange, uncomfortable situation.

One night about a week later, I did something that I still find hard to believe: I called the head of Arthur Andersen & Co. at his home to find out if he had received my letter. I hadn't heard anything back, and I was afraid that my letter may not have been given to him. His wife, who answered my call, sounded pleasant and helped arrange a time for me to talk with her husband the following day.

Early the next morning, the head of the firm called me in my hotel room. "I received your letter," he said, "and I want to thank you for taking the time to apprise me of the situation." His voice sounded kind but noncommittal.

"I didn't know what to do," I said. "I know this project won't be done on time."

"I'd prefer not to discuss the project at this time, but I give you my word ... I will look into it."

He gave no indication as to whether he believed me or thought I was some crazed woman having trouble with her job. In truth, I did feel as if my sanity was in question as I continued to sit imprisoned in the partner's office day after day.

One day about a month later, the partner didn't show up at "our" office, and an announcement was made that a different partner would take over the project.

My desk was moved back into a regular cubicle, but I still felt quite uncomfortable. I felt shunned by my male coworkers and occasionally received antagonistic looks from some of them. Consequently, I decided to put in a request to the corporate HR department of my firm to be transferred elsewhere.

Four months later, after I had completed the initial design of the inventory control and distribution systems, I sat down in my manager's office to receive my performance evaluation. I was scheduled to leave Kansas City the following morning for a new assignment.

I didn't know what to expect when my manager leaned across his desk and nonchalantly handed me my review. I quickly scanned the evaluation and found it to be very favorable, except for a brief comment about my tendency to act in an insubordinate manner.

"Could you explain this comment about insubordination?" I asked, astonished he had the nerve to put such a thing in my evaluation, given how I had been treated.

"You didn't have to blow the whistle, Donna. Things would have worked out in their own good time."

"Well, what did you expect me to do after you ordered me to do something impossible, and then tried to intimidate me by putting me in the partner's office?"

"You should have stayed calm and done your job without causing a problem."

Although I knew that arguing with him was futile at that point, I reflected on how I had handled the situation. There was no doubt that I had been extremely angry and upset when I was given my unreasonable timeline, and even more so when my desk was moved into the partner's office. Who wouldn't have been? Would the partner have tried to intimidate a man in the same way? There had to be many men on this project who knew it wouldn't cutover on time, I reasoned, but they hadn't felt compelled to do anything about it. Maybe they were afraid of losing their job if they said anything. Or maybe it was because men are raised to be team players and support each other, even when they know they are wrong.

I knew that I had a rebellious streak, which tended to show up if anyone tried to put me down or put me in my place. I had gained much experience as a young child by rebelling against my father's controlling ways.

In the first grade, I was expelled from school one day because my teacher, who was a nun, had scolded me for completing exercises ahead of the class in my *Jolly Number* arithmetic book and I talked back. I remember getting up from my desk after listening to her disapproving remarks, marching to the front of the classroom, standing with my hands on my little hips, and loudly calling her a black witch. I stayed home for several days after that, because I refused to apologize—the condition for being allowed back into school. Only the sight of my mom upset and crying for days caused me to finally agree to go to school and reluctantly apologize.

When I entered the business world, I noticed that my female colleagues also seemed to have that stubborn, rebellious tendency. Perhaps we needed that attitude to survive.

The partner in charge of the project in Kansas City was correct in fearing I would blow the whistle. But I may not have done so if he hadn't incarcerated me in his office. The experience seemed almost surreal to me. It didn't fit what I considered to be normal behavior in a business environment. Perhaps that was part of my problem—I didn't yet understand how abnormal the business world can be. But if survival in the business world depended upon ignoring irregularities and red flags, and focusing on the job at hand, I couldn't do that. Later in my career, I would earn the nickname "Corporate Conscious" because some coworkers saw me fight against corporate wrongdoings and fight for employees and customers.

Of course, men can be intimidated too, but people tend to bully those who are smaller in physical stature or lower in position—characteristics that often apply to women. As I later learned, someone may try to make me angry or try to intimidate me, but it's up to me whether I choose to become angry or intimidated. I can assure you, however, that it wasn't my imagination that the partner meant to intimidate me by having my desk moved into his office. And, as I suspected from the start, the project in Kansas City took two and a half more years to complete.

Looking back, I'm glad I did what I did. Being told to not tell the client the truth about the project's progress and extreme intimidation were the catalysts; I had reached my limit of abuse. What is amazing about this story is that the head of such a large, prominent firm, Arthur Andersen & Co., would acknowledge and listen to one of his lowliest subordinates.

Every woman should decide her limit for any kind of intimidation or abuse. We know from stories about prominent people that abuse and intimidation are still rampant in our society. As recent as 2021, women described an intimidating and abusive atmosphere that Andrew Cuomo, then governor of New York, engendered while in office, in addition to alleged sexual harassment. Unfortunately, as women have risen in power, some of them, too, have learned how to intimidate and bully.

As my career progressed, I experienced many other times when men tried to bully me into silence or force me into supporting their point of view. I would feel threatened, but sometimes did remain silent, unless I felt strong and emboldened that day and had facts to refute his position.

To this day, I shudder when I remember one man who had fine-tuned the art of intimidation. He was a manager for IBM, and I was the client representative for a computer software project. This time the system being developed was not only late, but I believed it would not work as intended. When sitting behind his big desk, refuting my analysis, and glowering at me over the rim of his glasses didn't work, he tried to discredit me with my boss. While my boss did question my judgment, I was correct about my analysis, and the project eventually failed and resulted in the loss of many millions of dollars for both companies.

○ ○ ○ ○

Human societies have intimidated females for eons—some countries and cultures obviously more than others. As little girls we learned how to shut down and evade repercussions, whether physical or psychological. So when faced with intimidation, we sometimes react as we did as a child. Fear takes over. As with so many other issues during my career, whenever I backed down and did not address an issue in a forthright manner, I felt less powerful and confident in myself. Certainly, intimidation was one of those issues.

There are many ways to address intimidation; sometimes just verbalizing the feeling of intimidation changes the dynamic of the conversation. I think of several situations when I could have said to a man: "I feel threatened by your tone of voice." That acknowledgement alone would have put me in a more powerful position, whereas disregarding the threat or menacing tone of voice only made me feel more vulnerable.

While verbal intimidation and bullying are often witnessed in today's society, on occasion the threats become physical. Something I realized about myself was that I had a subconscious fear of men doing physical violence to me. Other than the sexual abuses I mentioned previously, I have only once experienced physical violence from any man. One night I was attacked while standing alone in a parking lot; a man threw me to the ground, scraped my face against the rough pavement, and then stole my purse. That incident had a profound, lasting psychological effect on me. Although I experienced verbal threats as a child from my father, who often threatened to throw me or my brother through a window, he never acted upon that threat. So why, I have asked myself, do I have this fear? Is it merely from that one incident in a parking lot, or childhood threats from my father?

Physical violence of any kind has always upset me. Sometimes men's loud voices, reddened faces, and combative stances put me on high alert. I remember hearing about the physical violence used by some priests at the high school that my brother attended. One time his best friend was battered and thrown against a locker. I was upset for days after hearing about that incident.

Being of small stature and weight for most of my life—five-foot-five and 120 pounds—I have always felt physically weaker than most men. I grew up in an era when men sometimes settled arguments by physically fighting. There was even an incident during my career when two rather large-sized, high-level male executives (both impeccably dressed in business suits and ties) fought each other in my enclosed office. One man cringed in pain as the other man bent his hand backwards, away from his wrist. I felt trapped and shaken, actually trembling as I watched them fight. Another time a volatile boss raised his arm as if to hit me, but stopped short of doing so.

As I reflect about my fear of men, I realize that it has many facets. As men have wielded power, they have subjugated women into submission by using both physical and verbal threats. The obvious result is that this abuse of power has made me angry. The not-so-obvious result is that it has caused me to be fearful of men: Most men could hurt me physically if they wanted to, and they were certainly effective in keeping me in my place for much of my career.

Many women who have been raised by soft-spoken, nurturing fathers may not have the same fear I do. My fear of physical violence is primarily a subconscious fear. I don't consciously think most men would hurt me physically. Moreover, I think physical violence is a rarity in the workplace today (at least, I hope it is). Yet I encourage women to consider learning self-protection techniques for two reasons: First, such knowledge could help in rare circumstances, whether work-related or otherwise; and second, prior generations of women have passed along this fear of violence from men—consciously or unconsciously. In fact, some studies suggest that trauma can be transmitted genetically from generation to generation.[8]

While physical violence in the workplace may be rare today, intimidation and bullying are commonplace. Fear is a disempowering emotion. Business schools would do well to teach both women and men how to handle the intimidation and bullying, which many will encounter in the workplace. I wish I had taken such a class.

FIVE

Responsibility Without the Title, Pay, or Promotion

Since the beginning of my business career, I had been dogged by unfair treatment in title and pay. I witnessed man after man promoted who did not have the breadth of my experience. What I didn't realize at the time (and something I hope all young women recognize now) is that when a woman starts her career being given a lower salary or title than her male peers, it is hard to catch up. Often, one's promotions are based on previous pay and pay grades. So the fact that I did not receive equal promotions and pay in my early career at the Big Eight firm made it hard for me to catch up to my peers. That said, one engagement became my breaking point.

After I'd accrued several years of successful computer design experience, the firm assigned me to develop a system for the management and dispersal of a state's unemployment benefits. The project would eventually be staffed with over one hundred people from our firm, but I and one other woman were the first consultants on the project. At that time it was unusual to have more than one female employee working in a key role of a given engagement for our firm. Between the two of us, Ruth and I were in charge of designing and writing the specifications for the entire system.

The importance of the project was highlighted by the fact that two high-ranking partners in charge of the project showed up daily at the government building. One of the partners, Bob, was an extremely bright, ambitious, yet ethical man, while the other partner was arrogant and seemed willing to do anything to get ahead. Fortunately for me, I was able to work most of the time with Bob. In fact, I worked much more closely with him on a daily basis than with my manager. Bob had a good understanding of my work, whereas my manager seemed to have no role to fulfill on the project, other than to sit at his desk and occasionally glance in my direction. Unfortunately for Ruth, she had to work with the other partner.

Several state lawyers had been assigned to assist me with the interpretation of the rules for unemployment eligibility and payments. Surprisingly though, the questions I asked of the state's lawyers usually went unanswered. When I told my manager about the lawyers' lack of responsiveness, he gave me a list of lawyers to contact in Washington, D.C. I soon found the Washington lawyers to be no more decisive than the state's lawyers.

○ ○ ○ ○

Ruth and I didn't have much time to talk informally because of our tight project deadlines. But one day she seemed extremely upset and asked me to go to the cafeteria with her for lunch. Normally, we just had a quick bite to eat at our desks. I was aware that Ruth had received her performance evaluation that morning.

"At first the review sounded pretty good," Ruth said. "He said I was doing an excellent job of designing my programs. As if he would know!" she added sarcastically. "Then he said I needed to work on my interpersonal skills." Tears welled up in her eyes and her lips trembled.

"What did he mean by that?"

"I don't know. I asked him to explain, and I think he took offense at my questioning him. He said I should know what he was talking about. Then he looked down at some papers on his desk, as if to dismiss me."

"That sounds pretty typical of him."

"I asked to see my personnel file, but he just ignored me. I could see my file with my name on it, sitting on his desk. So I leaned over the front of his desk and grabbed it."

"Wow! That was pretty brave of you," I said, as I sat back in my chair, imagining the reaction of her arrogant boss. "What did he say?"

"He grabbed my wrist and squeezed it hard until I dropped my file. Then he told me not to ever do that again. I felt like I was going to start crying, so I left his office."

"What are you going to do now?"

"I'm going to corporate personnel and demand to see my file."

I didn't think Ruth should have grabbed her file from the partner's desk like that, but I understood the frustration that led her to do such a thing.

Although Ruth was a very smart, competent computer analyst, she did not project a feminine image. She had a short boyish haircut, wore little makeup, and projected a no-nonsense, businesslike persona. I believed that she was being penalized for her appearance, as well as her strong personality. I suspected that I was also being maligned as well, but for my much more feminine image—my long blonde hair, stylish dresses, and softer personality. I feared I wasn't seen as being businesslike enough—that is, not masculine enough.

What was the proper image for a woman in business? I wondered. Although there weren't many differences in the way businessmen dressed (except some of their ties were flashier or drabber than others), they seemed to get away with exhibiting the full range of their personalities—from serious to humorous—and they still got promoted.

Ruth and I were upset because we hadn't been promoted to the same levels as most of our male peers had been, even though we were given important responsibilities that were usually more difficult and critical to an engagement than the jobs of our peers and many of our superiors. We had been given small promotions at a much slower pace. The fact that Ruth reported directly to a partner was highly unusual and certainly a distinction worthy of promotion. Usually an employee at our firm had to be at least a manager to have that kind of reporting relationship.

At first I blamed my lack of promotion on not having an MBA degree, although many male technical consultants with experience comparable to mine had been promoted without an MBA. Furthermore, I was well on my way to obtaining an MBA, a fact I had let my bosses and HR know.

As I look back, it's hard to believe that Ruth and I ever wasted our energy on trying to figure out what we were lacking ... it was a penis. We just continued to work as hard as we could, giving our hearts and souls to the job. And staying true to my optimistic nature, I continued to believe I would eventually be recognized for my work.

o o o o

After weeks of not getting the answers I needed to write the specifications for the unemployment system, from either the state or Washington lawyers, I knew I had a choice to make: either I interpreted the rules for unemployment eligibility and compensation myself, or I allowed the project to be late. The challenge was to pick the best legal description from the hundreds of books available in the state's unemployment offices. I chose the most current, easy-to-understand book I could find and used as my guiding principle whatever I thought was fair for both employers and employees. Although I documented my decisions (so I couldn't be accused of operating on my own), I asked myself, who in their right mind would give a junior consultant without a legal background that kind of decision-making authority for what thousands of people would be paid?

Nevertheless, based upon my legal interpretations, I designed the system and wrote the specifications. Before I knew it, sixty programmers were assigned to program the specifications I had written. And guess who ended up having the responsibility for supervising them? Without being explicitly told to do so, the programmers started coming to me directly with their questions. Eventually, my manager asked me to write a brief paragraph about the performance of all sixty of them. That was usually the manager's job, but he said I should do it because I was the one closest to their work. Somehow these additional responsibilities steadily evolved.

While my manager sat at his desk every day and did nothing (for all I could see), the partners walked the halls, wringing their hands. I imagine they were worried that the project would not be done on time.

Although I was committed to ensuring the project was successful, underneath my calm exterior, I felt rage building up inside of me. Here I was, a junior consultant, practically running a multimillion-dollar project, doing everything from legal analysis to computer design to management supervision. You would think someone would have done something to promote me, wouldn't you? I couldn't even allow myself to think about the unfairness of my compensation because, needless to say, pay was reflective of title and position. I was so angry that I don't know how I managed to think rationally at that job, but obviously I kept my head together, because more and more work was piled on top of me.

I look back on the situation and wonder: Why didn't I go to the HR department at the corporate office and demand to be promoted or threaten to quit, instead of plugging along, seething with anger and waiting to be promoted? Or why didn't I tell my manager or one of the partners in charge of the project that I was going to quit if I wasn't immediately promoted, which surely would have made the project cutover late? That probably would have been even more effective than going to HR. But then, what would have happened once the project was completed? Would there have been other repercussions?

I now feel embarrassed about my inaction and find it hard to believe that I did nothing on my own behalf. But this tendency to not stand up for oneself was an issue for many women of my era; many of us thought (perhaps at a subconscious level) that our rights and our desires were not as important as those of our male counterparts. We had been taught through the example of our mothers and the other women who served as role models during our childhood to play a secondary, lesser role than men. We were psychologically conditioned and trained to be efficient but docile helpmeets, supporting our men in the important work of running the world. Those ingrained social paradigms and gender biases run deep.

In addition, as one of the first women in technical consulting, I felt great pressure to be successful—not only for myself, but for future generations of women. I felt I had been given an honor, and I didn't want to blow it by complaining or making demands. Unfortunately, not standing up for myself was a mistake I made throughout my career.

∘ ∘ ∘ ∘

One night, about one in the morning, my phone rang in my apartment. It was Bob, my partner on the engagement. To my mind, a high-level partner calling a junior consultant at home in the middle of the night reinforced the inappropriateness of my position.

"Donna, I want you to come in and help us debug a computer program," Bob said.

"I don't know anything about the actual programs," I answered. "Between writing the specs and supervising the programmers, I haven't seen the code. Also, it's been ages since I've done any programming."

"I know. But the entire system test is hung up, waiting for this program to be debugged."

"Can't you get some of the hotshot programmers in there?" I asked angrily. "I'm sure they could debug the program better than I could."

"We've already tried that. We've had five guys in here since early evening, and they're not making any progress. I thought a fresh set of eyes might help, particularly since you understand what the program is supposed to do."

"Well, I couldn't get in there right away anyway. My hair is wet." I had set my towel-dried hair in rollers after washing it and had been too tired to sit under the hood of my dryer for a half hour or more. In 1976, hand-held hair dryers were not generally in use, or at least I didn't have one.

"We don't have time for you to dry your hair," Bob said. "Please, just throw a scarf over your head and get in here as soon as you can. This is really important to me. I have to give a report to the client first thing in the morning."

"Okay," I said. "I'll be there shortly."

Perhaps that was the time when I should have negotiated for a promotion and higher pay. But I didn't. I liked and respected Bob, and didn't want him to get in trouble.

I quickly pulled the rollers out of my hair, got dressed, and drove to the government office. After several hours of working with the programmers, we found the problem in the code. By the time it was fixed, it was daylight, and there I was, running my fingers through my limp, straight hair, as I greeted my colleagues coming into work. That morning was my breaking point. I decided to leave the firm at my first opportunity. I felt defeated and abused. I couldn't take the unfair treatment anymore.

Surprisingly, the opportunity for another position arose several days later. A manager from one of my previous clients called to talk to me about a job, and I accepted the position after a brief interview. It was a rash move, and I knew I should have interviewed with other companies, but I felt too beaten down and burnt out to continue interviewing.

Bob immediately sought me out when he heard I was leaving. "Donna, I understand why you want to leave," he said, "but don't just take the first offer that comes your way. You could have many opportunities with your skill and experience. Just think about it. I'm not trying to talk you into staying, but I want you to do the right thing for yourself."

I would always remember Bob's supportive words and frequently wondered if I should have listened to his advice and not taken the first job that happened my way. I also wondered why Bob himself didn't think of promoting me, because he surely had the power to do so.

In those days most men, whether they thought women were capable or not, just couldn't picture women in managerial positions. That would mean women would have to give orders to men—a total role reversal.

Women were already starting to become managers in the tax and accounting divisions of the firm. Perhaps that was threatening enough.

In spite of Bob's advice, I feared I would start screaming if I had to face one more incident of unfair treatment. I needed to leave the firm as soon as possible for my own survival and sanity.

Upon hearing the news of my resignation, the other partner on the engagement called the client who had offered me the job and tried to talk him out of hiring me. The client fortunately did not acquiesce, but told me later about the call. It was just one more of those bizarre business situations that I found hard to believe.

o o o o

I wanted to be sure the installation of the unemployment system was successful. To that end, I made the start date at my new company contingent on the successful implementation of the unemployment system, which was near at hand, and had assured everyone that I would be available by phone for assistance if there were any problems. I felt confident the system would work well.

Before leaving Arthur Andersen & Co., two things happened that I will always remember; they helped me to get over some of my anger and bitterness, and made me realize that the discrimination I had experienced was obvious to many.

The first incident involved the head of the firm. He was a very powerful man, but he was also one of the kindest and most ethical men I had ever known. Unlikely as it may seem, given my low-level position, I had talked to him on multiple occasions—the first time being after I wrote that letter about the project in Kansas City. I had identified discrimination as my reason for leaving the firm on an exit-interview form, and he had requested to see me. I had agreed to the meeting out of respect for him.

On the day of our meeting, he stood and greeted me with a warm smile as I walked into his large office and sat down.

"I can't tell you how disappointed I am, Donna, to hear you are leaving the firm," he said. Then he offered me a glass of water and took his time pouring it, which made me feel as if he had all the time in the world to talk to me.

"I had surely hoped we would have made more progress by now in incorporating women into our firm," he said, after sitting back down in his chair. "I can assure you we are planning to increase our efforts."

I listened politely but didn't say anything.

"I'd like to make a proposal to you," he continued, "but I don't expect you to believe me or anyone else, so everything I say would be put in writing—you know, just in case I get hit by a train or something."

We both smiled. *If only everyone could be like him*, I thought.

"My proposal is that we immediately make you a manager and guarantee that you receive specific promotions and raises for the next two years, no matter what your performance is. Of course, I know it will be stellar. After that, I hope we will have become progressive enough that your career can follow a normal path. You are an exceptional talent, Donna, and we don't want to lose you."

I considered his offer for only a brief moment before responding. "I am flattered by your offer, but I don't think I should accept it. Although I love the work of the firm and have learned so much, I think too much has happened for me to stay. My negative feelings over how I've been treated will be difficult for me to overcome. I think it's best for me—and the firm—if I leave and get a new start. But I greatly appreciate your generous offer."

A year or so earlier, I would have jumped at his offer ... but it was too late. I felt weary, and my heart was heavy. I wanted to forget all about my unfair lack of promotion and unequal pay and, hopefully, overcome my anger at how I had been treated. Anger can be such a draining emotion, and anger is a normal reaction to being treated in an inferior manner.

I suspected that my negative feelings about my failure to advance at the firm were intensified because of the complex relationship I had with my father. In spite of his domineering, controlling ways, he had always told me I would be successful at whatever I did. His confidence in me had never waned. So the fact that I hadn't succeeded, at least not to the same extent as my male colleagues in terms of position and pay, was difficult for me to accept. More than anything, I wanted to forget my resentment and start over.

It didn't occur to me at the time that the reason the head of the Big Eight firm might be making me such an attractive offer was because he was afraid of a gender discrimination lawsuit. I was still too naïve to even think such a thing. I sincerely believed he was just trying to help me because he liked me and thought I was a good performer. Believe it or not, I still feel that was the case—that he was sincerely trying to help me because he liked me and thought I had talent.

o o o o

The second heartwarming incident happened on the day I left the firm. During my last two weeks at the government agency, many of my colleagues had congratulated me on my new job. That was just common courtesy and normal office procedure.

On my last day, however, as I started walking out of my office toward the elevator, a standing ovation of almost one hundred, mostly male colleagues followed me; some of them had witnessed my unfair treatment for years. They clapped loudly as I stood there at the elevator, carrying a box of my belongings and waiting for the doors to open. That was not normal procedure. I saw Brad smiling and clapping in the crowd. No words needed to be spoken. My colleagues and clients were applauding me for having the courage to move on. Tears came into my eyes as I walked into the elevator. And then when the doors shut, I let the tears roll down my face.

o o o o

It was many years before I could put my treatment on that project to rest and forgive my perceived persecutors. Imagine how terrible my manager must have felt, sitting there day after day, watching me work while he had nothing to do. As for the two ambitious partners on the job, I don't think they even noticed the unfairness of the titles that Ruth and I had been given. The fact that their fate rested on two women to do the job properly must have been discomforting for both of them. Obviously, one handled his feelings better than the other.

Although I had heard the phrase "power corrupts," I was beginning to witness firsthand how that transpires in the corporate world. In my previous assignments, as well as on that engagement, men who hadn't proved themselves in business were given opportunities to lead important projects. If successful, they could see themselves as top leaders in the future, with all the wealth and power that success assures. Years later, both of the partners on that project started hugely successful firms of their own. To go from a rather unknown, average Joe to someone with everything money can buy would be such a temptation that it is easy to see how anyone could get hooked by power and greed.

I wondered if the same thing could happen to me. Could I be seduced by power and success and be at risk of losing my ethical beliefs? I hoped not. I hoped I would be like the managing partner of the Big Eight firm who represented integrity, wisdom, and kindness. Like him, I hoped I would be a supporter of women and other minorities.

I empathize with all women who are struggling as to whether to continue facing discrimination in their current job or to resign. It's easy in hindsight to look back and think I should have resigned from the Big Eight accounting firm sooner than I did. But there are so many factors to consider when a woman is planning her next move. For one, women know that discrimination is rampant in most companies, or there would be far more female CEOs and less of a wage gap. There is no guarantee that the next firm will be any better. Gaining experience before moving on is another factor. Sometimes, just having a steady paycheck to put food on the table is an overwhelming consideration. So deciding when or when not to leave a job is a personal, often difficult, decision—one that many women are now struggling with because of the Covid-19 pandemic.

I encourage all women, however, not to let discrimination diminish their self-esteem. I realize I have said this before, and will continue to do so for emphasis. Just because the patriarchy has perpetuated gender discrimination for ages does not mean women aren't better businesswomen and leaders than men. Maintaining self-confidence will enable a woman to reach her full potential, in spite of any temporary decisions she may make.

SIX

Support and Lack of Support (or Worse)

Putting my past disappointments behind me, I stepped into my job at my new company, United Airlines, with a fresh outlook. Now that I was close to completing my MBA, I looked forward to a brighter, more successful future. I was also excited about living in one place and having more time for leisure interests. My many out-of-town assignments had been difficult on my social life. In fact, soon after I started my new job, I began dating Ralph, my future husband.

My first assignment as a senior team leader (still not a manager) was easy compared to my previous jobs. Within a year, Jack, the man who had hired me, became my ardent supporter and mentor. He promoted me to manager after the success of my first project. For the first time in my business career, I felt relaxed enough to have fun at work. I didn't feel so angry.

Jack, however, had an explosive temper. He seemed barely able to contain himself if anyone crossed him, and his tirades were legendary. A colleague told me a story about one time when a vendor had failed to deliver on an important project for Jack. At a meeting with the vendor representatives, he climbed on top of the long conference table and crawled on his hands and knees toward the men sitting at the other end of it, shouting angrily and berating them for their failure to deliver. I laughed about that story until my sides hurt and never got tired of hearing it told. Though Jack could be loud and bullying (even resorting to physical violence), I was never terribly afraid of him, because I knew I could do no wrong in his eyes. One time I decided to deliberately incite him—just for fun—just to see him react. This was a bit devilish, I admit, but I knew he would become agitated no matter how I confronted him about his estimates that I considered to be too low. Rather than pussyfoot around the issue, I marched into his office and stood next to his desk.

"Jack, your estimates are too low," I said in a strong voice, knowing that would be enough to make him go ballistic. No one challenged Jack.

"What do you mean?" he asked, as I watched his face getting red.

"They should be fifteen percent higher."

"I know my estimates are always correct."

"No … they're not," I said, in a firm voice. Then I turned around and ran out of his office as fast as I could. I held my hand over my mouth as I tore through the hallway, giggling all the way to the ladies' restroom. I knew he would have lost control of himself and would try to run after me. But I doubted that even he would have enough nerve to barge into the ladies' room.

He didn't find me until later that evening … after he had had time to cool down and get a hold of himself. Then we were able to have a civil conversation about his estimates. Although most of my male bosses were not as volatile as Jack, I had learned it was sometimes best to diffuse an argument by getting out of an eruptive person's space until they cooled off.

Almost forty years later, I often thought of Jack whenever I heard President Trump talk and tweet. They both got riled so easily and spoke as if they were experts on so many issues, whether they knew anything about the topic or not. Underneath their bluster, I sensed fear and a lack of confidence.

○ ○ ○ ○

Another senior executive named George, whom I admired for both his business knowledge and general wisdom, had taken note of my career. One night George and I sat talking afterhours in his office, as we often did.

"You know, Donna," George said, "there are a lot of things in the business world that are hard for me to take. Believe it or not, my stomach is upset most of the time at work. The things I see some of these executives say and do around here make me sick. All we can do is to try to do our best and maintain our integrity."

I knew that George had studied at one time to be a priest and I wondered if that experience had given him his strong, ethical foundation. George looked pensive, as if trying to decide whether to tell me something or not, and then continued talking.

"I've been thinking about asking you to lead a high-profile, complex project to develop a computer scheduling system under my direction. It will require working with various organizations in the States and internationally. I'm sure I will get some raised eyebrows for putting a woman in charge, but I am willing to take that risk. The project will be fraught with politics, because many organizations will try to protect their turf and undermine its success."

Then he went on to explain some details about the project.

"I would consider it to be an honor to lead the effort," I said, after he had finished. By now, the late1970s, I had been hoping the company's senior management would be open to allowing me to lead the project.

Several days later, wearing my best navy-blue suit that had shoulder pads in the jacket (which always made me feel more powerful), I walked into the office of the vice president who would be in charge of the project from the user side of the company and sat in a chair across from him. He was an elderly man with snowy-white hair.

"Well, young lady, they tell me you're very capable," the vice president said. "It's hard to imagine how an attractive young woman like you, who doesn't look to weigh more than one hundred pounds, can do a job like this."

"I know I can do it well, sir."

"All right then, I'll give you the chance. But you'd better do a good job, or I will be after you," he said, and then winked at me.

"Thank you, sir. You will not be sorry for giving me this opportunity."

Although he talked to me as if I was a little girl, his comments didn't really bother me. I suspected he would have treated a young man in a similar, fatherly fashion.

For me, there was a difference between how someone like him, from an older generation, acted and a younger man who should know how to talk to women as equals. I didn't think the vice president was being patronizing; rather, I felt he was trying to be supportive of me in his own, old-fashioned way.

The project was initiated, and I was given free rein to recruit any of the thousands of qualified people within the company or to hire from outside the company. What a team of superstars I put together! I couldn't have asked for a more hardworking, intelligent group of men and women. Although the two leaders of the project were men, I was able to staff the project with many technically-talented women.

o o o o

We worked around the clock for two years, with a second team working through the night so we could cut the original time estimate of four years almost in half. I usually worked during the day shift, but conducted a conference call with the second shift around midnight each night.

Though my husband, Ralph, and I had only recently married, he understood the necessity for the long hours I worked and how important the project was to both me and my company. He was a computer executive himself and had decided early on in our marriage that I was the one who had a better chance of climbing higher in the corporate ranks. Because he cooked dinner for the two of us almost every night and took care of most of our household chores, I was able to work late and still have some quality time with him when I got home.

I didn't realize (or perhaps appreciate enough) at the time how important it is for executives—and especially female executives—to have a supportive spouse. Without Ralph's support, I don't think I could have made it to the levels I eventually did. One of my most important pieces of advice for women who want to have a business career and family is to choose their partners wisely. And, if having children is important to a woman, then she needs even more support for daily chores and caregiving. Too much time and energy are required to climb the corporate ladder to also have to fight battles on the home front.

○ ○ ○ ○

My staff and I poured our hearts and souls into the project that George had assigned me to lead. Though George was responsible for the project overall, he kept his distance and let me manage the project as I saw fit, while giving me support whenever I needed it.

The lead manager from the user side of the project was a woman named Hilda. She was in her early sixties and was highly regarded by senior management. She was the toughest-acting woman I had ever known. I made sure we got along well and thought we had reached a point of mutual respect.

As often happens with computer projects, our project encountered some problems near its conclusion. One day my lead analyst told me we would not be able to capture all of the historical data that the specifications had called for. He said to capture the data would be a difficult manual task that would delay the project for at least a year.

I immediately called Hilda and explained the situation. She didn't seem too surprised or upset and told me we could easily work around the problem. So when George called me into his office several days later and showed me a memo she had written to the company's top executives, I was shocked. Her letter implied that the project had been mismanaged and was in serious jeopardy.

After reading the letter, I burst into tears.

"Donna, I've told you how important it is for women not to cry at work," George said, frowning with concern. "I know that might not be right, but that's how it is. I want you to stop crying while I respond to this letter."

"How could she do this without even talking to me?" I asked, as I continued to cry.

"What she should or shouldn't have done is not the issue now. You need to stop crying," George said calmly.

"I can't."

"What do you mean, you can't?" George folded his arms and eyed me over the rim of his glasses, as if I had said something incomprehensible to him.

"I mean … I can't," I sobbed. "I don't cry very often, but when I do, I usually don't stop crying for a long time."

"Well, this time you have to. You need to act as if everything is fine. The fallout from this letter will happen right away. Go into my projection room until you can get control of yourself."

I went into the small room next to his office and sat down on the floor, pulling my knees into my chest and resting my head on my folded arms. I felt so tired from working such long hours for two years, staying up late night after night to be on conference calls. Hilda's betrayal hit me as if my best friend had stabbed me in the back.

About ten minutes later, George opened the door. I was still sitting on the floor, but my crying had become more subdued. I looked up at him as tears continued rolling down my face.

"She is going to retract her letter and put out another one," he said. "She'll explain why it's not imperative to have all the historical data."

"The damage is already done," I said angrily. "Everyone is going to believe her first letter."

"It's not important. It's only important that you stop crying."

I stayed in the projection room until I felt I had control of my emotions.

Then, although my face was tearstained, I walked back to my office and forced myself to call Hilda. She acknowledged the inappropriateness of her letter and agreed, as she had previously, that the lack of historical data was not a critical issue.

When the project was completed several months later, the system was proclaimed to be highly successful. I even received a top award for my team's accomplishment. Yet in spite of the recognition, I believed the first letter that Hilda had written had tarnished my reputation.

I think there are a couple of important lessons in this story: The first is the damage that women can do to each other; and the second is the unacceptability of crying in the workplace.

In regard to the first issue, it's likely that Hilda was not trying to hurt me; she was probably just trying to protect herself in case someone else found the lack of historical data to be unacceptable. Nevertheless, I thought she could just as easily have raised her concerns to her boss, instead of putting the blame in writing for all the top executives of the company to see. Or she could have talked to my boss before writing the letter. Any of a number of actions would have been less damaging to my reputation as well as to my team's morale. Furthermore, I was the first woman in the company to be given such responsibility. How could she not have known that her letter would hurt me and the cause of all women?

I also wondered whether she would have written the letter in the same way if I had been a man. Although I didn't think women should be more lenient toward each other than they were toward men, I hoped they wouldn't be harder on each other either ... but sometimes they were.

Women backstabbed and hurt each other for one simple reason: the unspoken rule that only a few women can reach the most senior positions in a company. This unstated rule caused fierce competition among women climbing to the top. That is not to say that competition wasn't fierce among men; it was. It's just that men have learned it pays to help each other, because that help might need to be reciprocated in the future; many women hadn't yet learned the value of helping each other.

The next issue is about crying, or the expression of strong emotion in a business setting. Early in my career, all of my mentors warned me to never cry, or at least to not let anyone see me crying. Although I was a very emotional person by nature, with discipline, I taught myself how not to cry. Yet a few times I couldn't help crying, especially after a painfully hard blow, such as when Hilda's letter put a black mark on my reputation. Even George, who had now become a close friend, seemed taken aback by my tears.

I wondered why crying was seen as such a weakness in women in business, when it seemed to be perfectly acceptable for sports stars and politicians to cry in public in front of millions of television viewers when they lost. No one seemed to think less of them for it. Perhaps the same standard should apply to women at work—crying should be viewed as an honest, acceptable display of emotion, and possibly even be valued. I'm not talking about excessive or inappropriate crying, but simply allowing it as a way for sincere emotions to surface and be expressed.

A female friend once told me that the reason men don't cry at work is that they look at their jobs as just being business. She said they don't take the inevitable slights and put-downs personally, whereas women take their work much more to heart. I'm not sure that is universally true, but I do think men are better at hiding their feelings. While my brother was taught as a young boy that crying was unmanly, I cried frequently at the slightest rebuff. Men are made to feel ashamed of their emotions, which I think is the main reason they don't cry on the job.

Another reason is that women—like minorities—are required to work at a level that is often superior to men's, just to be taken seriously. Likewise, any criticism of their work is exponentially more damaging. It was a blow to my pride, since I knew I had done a superlative job on the project, to be betrayed by a colleague this way, especially a female colleague who would well know the impact her letter could cause. A man receiving such a letter might not feel all that injured; but for me, tears were in order.

After that project, I vowed to be wary of other females in the workplace, particularly if they were in positions of power. I also vowed to never cry at work again. Slowly, I was conforming to what was expected of me in the business world.

○ ○ ○ ○

Certainly as I was climbing the corporate ladder, there was an unspoken understanding that a limited number of women could be promoted to senior jobs. I think there was a fear that promoting women would take away advancement from men (which would be true), and perhaps, more important, that those in charge did not want to see the senior ranks infested and run by hysterical, emotional women.

One would think, as women gained more education and experience, that some of this antiquated thinking would have changed. Given the difficulty for a woman to become successful, one might think the time of women being critical and prejudicial toward each other or bullying their female colleagues in the workplace would be over. Susannah Wellford, an opinion contributor for *U.S. News* and a leader of a national political organization to help women get elected, wrote in 2016 that she would place women not helping each other as one of the top ten reasons impeding women's success. "When I speak to women around the world about barriers to leadership, I consistently hear that other women are their worst enemies,"[9] Wellford wrote.

In addition to women fighting each other at work, they often hold prejudicial attitudes about each other; some even think women aren't as capable as men. Sometimes female employees will demonize another woman when she acts assertively and strives to get ahead in a competitive business environment, or respond with jealousy or bitterness toward another woman's achievement. Consequently, the only fair conclusion is that it's not only men who hinder women's progress.

I admired those few women who managed to get ahead in the companies where I worked. To my mind, they were clearly smarter than most of their male colleagues. I reasoned that they had to be smarter and work harder to be promoted and fend off constant attacks by colleagues.

At the same time, I also pitied the majority of women I saw in dead-end jobs that required few brains to complete their monotonous tasks—like data entry and some secretarial duties. I would walk down the halls of my company and see massive numbers of women chained to these repetitive, mindless tasks. For the most part I was just grateful for the jobs I had.

Years later I was confronted with a situation that made me further evaluate my attitude toward women. I was informed that I would need surgery to remove several uterine tumors that might be cancerous. Through a series of referrals, I was scheduled to be operated on by a female surgeon.

Although I did not verbalize any disappointment at the time, I knew in my heart of hearts that I wished the surgeon was a man. Perhaps if I hadn't been so frightened and upset, my reaction might have been different. Perhaps if the surgery had been a minor operation, I would have accepted having a female surgeon more readily. But the truth is, I would have preferred a male surgeon for my operation—so I had to acknowledge my discomfort and decide what I wanted to do about it.

After doing some research, I discovered that my female doctor had an exceptionally positive reputation as a surgeon. She had also earned a reputation for not having a good bedside manner, but in that regard, she had something in common with many of her male colleagues. After further soul-searching, I decided to keep her as my surgeon.

In the weeks that followed, after she misdiagnosed a complication from my exploratory surgery and failed to perform proper follow-up procedures, I decided I could no longer abide by my original decision. This time I felt confident my decision was not based on gender, but strictly on her competence and business practices.

The specifics of my surgery are not important here. What is important is that I had an initial, less-than-enthusiastic response to having a female surgeon without knowing anything about this doctor's reputation or her performance history. To say that my prejudicial view was shocking to me is an understatement, after all my talk about giving women equal opportunity. A woman as a surgeon was okay, as long as that doctor wasn't performing surgery on me.

When under stress or duress, we tend to slide back into old beliefs and comfort zones. At some point in my upbringing, I must have gotten the message that men make better surgeons than women. Easy enough to believe, since all the doctors I knew when I was growing up were men.

Then, to assuage my guilt over my negative reaction to having a female surgeon, I allowed her to make more mistakes than I would ever have tolerated from a man before changing doctors. Although her performance as a doctor was totally unacceptable, I tried to stick by her. Furthermore, whenever I met with her, she looked and acted exhausted. Perhaps her fatigue had contributed to her misdiagnosis and lack of follow-through.

As I struggled with my discriminatory feelings, I sat down to talk with a friend who was a retired nurse and who tended to be quite blunt.

"I definitely prefer a male surgeon over a female one," she said emphatically, after I told her about my experience.

I didn't respond, although I was somewhat surprised by her categorical statement.

"Women have to work so much harder than men," she said, "and there are so many distractions along the way. A man just has to get up in the morning, put on his shirt and tie, and walk out the door. He can focus on his job and not be bothered by all of the issues that invariably distract women—like kids and other family matters."

I just stared at my older friend. She had stated so succinctly the exact thoughts I had been having but did not want to acknowledge.

"And then, how do you know if your female surgeon will not be feeling well because of hormonal changes during those few days every month?" she asked. "Plus, I can't tell you the number of women doctors I saw struggling during their last months of pregnancy to continue their practices. I am not prejudiced; these are facts based upon many years of seeing women practice medicine."

Although I was disturbed by the inflexibility of her statements, I knew that my own views were not much different. I think that many—maybe most—people don't believe themselves to be prejudiced, until something or someone directly challenges their belief and makes them see it. Most of us follow the "live and let live" philosophy of life.

This unexpected surgery triggered a whole host of unwanted feelings and thoughts about my own beliefs. I felt ashamed that I had ever considered men to be the only ones holding prejudices against women.

After that experience, I decided to become more aware of any discriminatory feelings I had, examine them, and hopefully choose wisely and make decisions not based on biased thoughts or feelings. I think that's all anyone can ask of themselves—to be aware and consider whether their reactions might be based on biases that were consciously or unconsciously developed a long time ago.

Another important lesson for me to learn was to not use that one negative experience and become dismissive of all female doctors. The same logic holds true for our business leaders—we must not see the performance of one woman who fails as indicative of all other women, or even of that woman all of the time.

Since women are still in the minority at the top of most professions, it is hard not to focus on their failures. By contrast, I know if I had met an incompetent male doctor, I would definitely not extend my bias to all male doctors. In addition, women are particularly vulnerable to criticism now that they are being tapped to rescue troubled companies.

The promotion of women to rescue a company is often referred to as the "glass cliff" phenomenon. This may be a reason why the percentage of female CEOs at Fortune 500 companies has jumped to 8% during the Covid-19 pandemic.

Business writers and analysts have offered many reasons these "glass cliff" nominations occur for women: Men may see the job as too risky and therefore decline the job offer for fear of failing; women may not be aware of the inherent risks of failure that men perceive; women may be offered the job because they are viewed as having the necessary skills to lead employees during difficult times; and boards may know the woman can be replaced with a man when she fails. Although all are plausible, I prefer to think that the primary reason for these "glass cliff" appointments is that women make better leaders … especially when a company is in trouble. Furthermore, there are a growing number of examples where women succeed in these difficult positions.

Throughout my career, I was often given tasks involving difficult, politically charged situations, usually requiring technical and broad knowledge. Sometimes the assignments involved calming disgruntled employees over unpopular stances taken by the company. Unfortunately, the successful completion of these assignments only aggravated my sense of injustice when I failed to receive a permanent position or promotion. I would urge women who take on these "glass cliff" assignments to negotiate upfront the reward for both success and failure, before accepting these high-risk positions.

o o o o

Discriminatory feelings against women are based on several additional factors. First, women are challenged more frequently as to their competency, which can cause them to feel somewhat inferior to men; this causes them to act overly confident in some situations or lacking in confidence at other times. Second, the minority quota system or perceived quota system that required a certain number of women be placed in various positions has put some women in positions where they may not be as competent or qualified as some men. Third, women often lack the necessary experience to be considered for the top jobs—especially for CEO positions.

Historically, women have tended to hold positions in staff versus operational line functions. Although staff functions, such as human resources, general business, accounting, and marketing are important, they don't necessarily prepare a person to run a company—or at least that is the perception. Most men will concede that women are better at handling certain aspects of business, such as counseling employees or encouraging collaboration, but they are skeptical about women's ability to make difficult decisions and manage a large corporation.

Sometimes women have difficulty attaining positions in operational areas, especially in areas that require physical strength. In some businesses, there is an unspoken undercurrent of thought that only males have the "balls" needed to handle the tough jobs and make critical decisions.

My point here is that one of the reasons women have been held back from CEO and other top positions is because they do not have the operational experience of how to run a company or an organization. This lack of experience, along with being viewed as the weaker sex, largely accounts for why women haven't attained a higher percentage of CEO positions. Yet things are quickly changing, and many more women are gaining the necessary experience to run companies and to assume top political positions as well.

Mary Barra at General Motors (GM) is a good example of someone who had both staff and line experience before becoming CEO. She was vice president of human resources until she was moved into global product development. She earned an electrical engineering degree and began work as a controls engineer in a GM plant. In other words, she gained valuable education and experience in multiple functions before becoming CEO.

The problem with all prejudice is that when someone holds onto a false belief about someone else based on a negative bias, it does not allow that person to be seen in a fair and objective light. Perhaps there was a time when women did not have the education or experience to be senior-level executives. Perhaps there was a time when women allowed their emotions to rule them, because that was how they were raised. But the situation has changed now that women have gained education and learned what is expected of them in the workplace. In all professions, there will be individuals with long-held beliefs that women are not as smart, strong, capable, logical, etc. as men. The first step to changing our beliefs is to be open to the possibility of change. More and more women will succeed in the business world when we honestly examine our prejudicial beliefs and allow women to thrive. Prejudice of any kind usually leads to discrimination.

The important thing to remember is that despite both men's and women's prejudicial views against women, progress has been made. And the most important point of all is that if we, as women, don't erase our prejudices against each other, then how can we possibly see ourselves as being equal to men and expect to be treated fairly?

○ ○ ○ ○

I was fortunate to have such a supportive spouse. And, although not my choice at the time, I was not able to conceive children. Therefore, I was able to devote much time and energy to my career. Women should not have to choose between a family and a career; men do not have to make that choice.

Since the new millennium, some companies have been trying to support women through innovative programs. KKR & Co., an investment firm, offered new parents perks, such as paying to fly nannies and infants on business trips during the baby's first year, and paying shipping costs to send the mother's breast milk home. KKR & Co. even offered unlimited coverage for fertility treatments.[10] Arizona Health Services allowed new parents—both mothers and fathers—to bring newborns to the office until they are six months old.[11] PricewaterhouseCoopers created a program called Full Circle, designed to keep new mothers up to date on happenings in the firm through coaching and training for up to five years while at home raising their children or providing care for elderly parents.[12]

While higher unemployment figures have been seen since the pandemic began for women in front-line roles in the food, healthcare, and retail industries, overall women gained in white-collar positions. According to the 2021 Women in the Workplace report by McKinsey & Leanin.Org.: "The proportion of women in the corporate workforce didn't decline significantly last year, and the number of women holding some senior level roles rose."[13] In addition, more women opted to start their own business. "Roughly half of people who started businesses in 2020 were women, up from 27% in recent years."[14]

Women who have left corporations during the pandemic (as well as those women considering doing so) should take another look at some of the innovative programs that progressive companies are instituting. "Facing a brain drain and labor shortages, some companies are responding not just by hiring more women with children. They're going to unusual lengths to assist mothers' re-entry into the workforce, address their desire for flexibility, and offer them more child-care support."[15]

PricewaterhouseCoopers continues to be an innovative company by monitoring promotions and questioning any group that they see lagging in promotions. Amazon.com Inc. recently made a huge commitment to women who have left the workforce by offering them paid returns, which are meant to attract stay-at-home moms and often result in permanent spots. Workhuman, an employee-engagement platform, recently hired a senior manager who started to work during her ninth month of pregnancy.

In the course of my research for this book, I have been very excited to conclude, from the programs being implemented for women, that many companies are really getting it. These are the kinds of programs women should be looking for if they want to attain a senior-level position and have a family. What I particularly like about these programs is that they are addressing the day-to-day, practical issues that women face, such as taking care of children.

There are now even conferences and consulting firms that give women advice. "Balance is not one-size-fits-all,"[16] says Aimee Cohen, a career coach and co-founder of Women on Point. She suggests that each woman define what works for her.

It's not only problems with children that challenge working women. Aging parents, ill partners, and other personal situations can give rise to the need for a woman to turn her attention to family members or friends. Most women view such situations as simply a part of life; but women are often looked down upon by their male colleagues for accepting any caregiver role and not placing business above personal issues.

When a man gives priority to family issues, the tendency is for workers to think of him both favorably and as an exception. By contrast, when a woman is faced with a family issue, there is a tendency to think that she should make a decision as to what's more important to her—career or family.

For most women, both career and family are important. Although some women maintain that it is difficult to have both, with planning, preparation, and the right kinds of support, it is possible to have both. Just as the good old boys had support from home and within their companies, women need the same kind of support (or more).

If companies want to be highly successful, they must figure out how to best support women. Much of that support must come from men; while forty-one women were CEOS at Fortune 500 companies in 2021, that leaves 459 companies run by men. Together, men and white female leaders must help all women, especially women of color, who lag significantly behind in most equality measures.

SEVEN

A Choice: Act Tough or Be Viewed as Weak

After my experience of breaking down and crying profusely in George's office, I tried to be less emotional at work. But the more I suppressed my emotions and distanced myself somewhat from my coworkers, the less of a warm and caring individual I must have seemed to my subordinates.

I noticed that many of my female colleagues who had reached higher levels in management appeared distant and unapproachable—often more so than their male counterparts. A perfect example of a woman who displayed this kind of aloof demeanor was Faye, who was in charge of a customer service department.

Faye was an attractive woman in her mid-forties, who wore expensive designer suits that looked fabulous on her slim figure. She almost never smiled. As I got to know Faye better, I realized that hiding behind her standoffish manner was a caring, sensitive woman. Although I single out Faye as an example, I knew many women who, like her, projected a tough demeanor—perhaps to protect themselves and detract from their feminine qualities.

I also noticed that even though these tough-acting women often instituted positive changes for their employees, as Faye did, they were not given due credit for their good works. Equally important, I came to realize that a woman who presents a tough image may inadvertently challenge her male colleagues to put her in her place. This is what I think happened to Faye.

Faye was in charge of overseeing about twelve thousand employees in her customer service department. Based on her past experience running large organizations, Faye was one of the most accomplished officers in my company. Yet when our company's profitability started to decline, I think some of her male colleagues saw an opportunity to demean her and deflect blame.

The company president had ordered Faye to cut substantial numbers of personnel in her department. Predictably, customer service levels plummeted, and more pressure was placed on the remaining employees in her department. Employee morale hit an all-time low, which caused customer service levels to drop even further.

I was frequently asked to sit in for my boss at the weekly officer meetings. During these meetings, each officer was supposed to explain variations from their business plans. Yet rarely was any officer actually required to comment on any shortfalls, financial or otherwise—except for Faye. Faye was asked to justify her department's performance at each and every meeting that I attended. I would watch in horror as Faye stood up in front of her male colleagues to make her presentation and, in my opinion, be crucified.

"Now, Faye, can you tell us why your customer service levels are so low?" asked the CEO, as he began grilling her at one of the meetings I attended.

"As I've told you before, and I will continue to tell you, there is a direct correlation between the number of personnel in my department and our customer service ratings," Faye answered calmly. "We are down hundreds of people, as was requested, and turnover is high. Employees are afraid they will be the next ones eliminated. There is no way we can expect service levels to increase unless we have more seasoned, experienced people on the phones."

"Perhaps you are not providing adequate training," said one of the vice presidents seated at the table.

"We are providing the same training as when our numbers were high. Furthermore, most of our customers now have to wait ten minutes or longer to speak to someone. That is another reason our numbers are low."

"What do you propose to do about the situation, Faye?" asked another senior vice president.

At that point, I think I would have screamed in exasperation, had I been Faye. Perhaps that was one of the reasons I wasn't an officer. Faye provided them with a solution every week (basically, to add more people), but no one seemed to want to listen. She had to stand up in front of the mostly male attendees seated at the conference table and defend herself, usually for at least a half hour. Perhaps if the company had established a culture where everyone was questioned and put through the third degree over poor performance, Faye's treatment would have been understandable. But no other officer was ever singled out. Millions of dollars could be lost, but the responsible executive would not receive an iota of the negative attention that Faye received.

Would Faye have been treated differently if she hadn't maintained such a tough demeanor? I wondered. Would the CEO and other officers have backed off from their repetitious questioning if Faye had shown signs of weakness during her weekly interrogation? Was Faye simply a scapegoat for the company's poor performance, particularly since she wasn't part of the good-old-boy network? I don't know. I just know it made me sick to witness Faye being persecuted.

After a year of harassment, I think Faye was asked to resign. Although I felt bad for her, I was happy that the inquisition, which I had found so painful to watch, was over.

○ ○ ○ ○

People's desire to see someone with a tough demeanor humbled seems universal, whether the individual is a man or a woman. I remember a reporter talking about the once brash CEO of WorldCom, Bernard Ebbers, being humiliated in a courtroom and reduced to tears after his sentencing over his company's huge accounting scandal.

In general, I don't think men feel the same compulsion to act tough as women do. By the very fact of being male, they are assumed to have inherent strength. Furthermore, a man who does not act tough is not necessarily perceived as weak; he might be considered wise, insightful, fatherly, or any number of other positive traits. Women who do not act strong are far more likely to be perceived as hesitant, indecisive, incompetent, and weak. The answer, however, in my opinion, is not for women to act tough.

Even though I was determined not to cry at work, I decided not to adopt a tough demeanor. I was aware that my decision could result in my being perceived as weak, but acting tough felt unnatural and false to me.

I also decided that acting tough externally had nothing to do with the ability to be tough when it came to making decisions. Time after time, I had seen executives (both men and women) talk tough, but then back down before making a difficult decision or fail to address issues in a forthright manner. I believed that one of my strengths was the ability to not only make difficult decisions, but also to stand by the consequences of those decisions.

As to my not defending Faye in the meetings I witnessed, I rationalized that I was there as an observer. I did not sit at the conference table; I was required to sit in a section designated for alternate representatives behind the conference table. I was just sitting in for my boss, and of course I had a much lower position and title than the participants. Those rationalizations were all copouts. I was in the room and should have come to Faye's defense … regardless of the circumstances or the potential consequences. My failure to do so is one of the things I am not proud of as I look back on my career.

I wish I had had the courage to stand up during one of those meetings when I had to sit on the sidelines, and say something like the following in a strong, clear voice: "Gentlemen, we all know that customer service is of paramount importance. But focusing on the consequences of the drastic cutbacks in that department week after week, and not addressing some of the other important issues in the company, is a mistake. In addition to customer service, we need to focus on revenue shortfalls, on-time performance, and employee morale. Insisting that Faye stand up here and rehash the same issue is not helping the overall health of this company. I implore you to start addressing these other critical issues, and stop what I see as persecution of Faye." I may have been trembling inside, but such a declaration would have boosted my confidence and possibly helped Faye.

Unfortunately, I was not able to do such a thing at the time. I let fear of making a fool of myself, and fear of being further excluded from the good-old-boys' club, stifle me. I hid behind the fear that such a declaration in Faye's defense would reignite a panic attack—something I had not experienced in many years. In hindsight, by taking such a stance, I may have gained respect and improved my standing with the executive team. I certainly would have felt better about myself.

∘ ∘ ∘ ∘

Although I had decided to not act tough, I never felt totally comfortable being myself in most situations where I was the only, or one of the few females in the room. Men's predominant style was to act dogmatic and domineering ... sometimes bullying. As I saw most of my female colleagues trying to imitate that style by acting tough and unemotional, I not only felt I was being perceived as weak, I actually felt weak. An exception was made for women in human resource positions; it seemed they were expected to be soft and yielding. But where did that leave me? It would be much, much later in my career before I was able to resolve this issue.

For women of today, I would say that demeanor and style are of paramount importance. First of all, let me say that if you are an extraordinarily brilliant woman, it makes no difference what you wear or how you say things—everyone will listen to you. I am talking about the super-bright person—someone like Katherine Johnson, the mathematician who helped the NASA space program in the 1960s. For a Black woman to be listened to and acknowledged for her mathematical calculations and insights in that male-dominated business in the sixties is nothing short of phenomenal!

Of the thousands of women I have known or supervised in my career, I would place only three in this stellar category. The first woman worked on the complex operating systems of early computers and had the most high-pitched, squeaky voice of any woman I have ever known; but believe me, when she talked all the men listened. The second was a fiery, crude-talking Latina who insulted and badmouthed most men; but because she always proffered a brilliant, innovative solution to any problem, everyone listened, and no one seemed to care about her insults and gutter language. And the third, although not as brilliant as the first two, had such remarkable insight and intuition that most everyone, especially the men she worked with, admired and respected her.

For most of us relatively smart, educated women, how we talk, dress, and act matters. The problem arises because adopting the tough, domineering, and dogmatic style of many businessmen does not work well for women and often causes pushback from men and other women.

Similar to the business world, many women in politics have modeled their style after the authoritative, exclusive, combative ways of the good-old-boys' club. A prime example, and one of the most prominent women in the history of American politics, is former Secretary of State Hillary Clinton, who ran for the presidential office in 2008 and 2016. There is no question that Clinton is smart, educated, experienced, and has many other positive attributes. But it was often said she didn't connect with people.

In a documentary about Hillary Clinton's life, she was portrayed as being somewhat introverted when she was younger. As her political career progressed, I suspect she was counseled to become more forceful, boastful, and strident to emulate the male model. By the end of the 2016 campaign, I would say that Clinton was doing a good job of demonstrating a masculine demeanor and style of speaking. I would say the same of

Carly Fiorina, another female presidential candidate who came across as tough and aggressive.

By contrast, Donald Trump was able to pull off a tough, bullying, command-and-control style and demeanor and get elected president. Although I am not applauding his style, he connected with many Americans, especially with many men, because of his domineering style and agenda of bygone eras. The female politicians at the time could not do the same, possibly because they were emulating a role that wasn't natural for them. These women actually seemed to garner more favor when they showed their vulnerabilities, as, for example, when Mrs. Clinton teared up one time during the 2008 presidential campaign. People still want to see men and women following traditional gender roles for behavior.

In 2020 Kamala Harris entered the U.S. national political stage. Although at times she came across as tough and dogmatic (perhaps demonstrating a style that she used in her legal profession), she also laughed a lot, even during the vice-presidential debate. She seemed to easily shrug off personal attacks, perhaps from having fended off years of discrimination as a Black and Asian woman in business and politics. Whether or not someone likes her or her politics, she is both strong and light-hearted, analytical and compassionate.

○ ○ ○ ○

A forceful male style does not work to the advantage of most women, because it usually comes across as objectionable. In fact, the masculine style of dominance, aggressiveness, and forcefulness is not very effective for many men in today's business world either—especially if the desired result is to obtain buy-in.

In many companies, the new style of leadership professes to be more inclusive, collaborative, and nurturing—attributes that many women possess, whether they are inherent or engendered by society. So why don't women demonstrate the use of these feminine skills? Because they don't want to appear weak? Because they have been told to act like men? Because they themselves have prejudices about women acting like women? Or is it that old fear that women want to be accepted in the good-old-boys' club, so they need to act like them?

This is not to say that women shouldn't stand up for themselves—for example, to negotiate for better pay, or speak up when treated disrespectfully or ignored in a meeting. Women must take the difficult stances and make the tough decisions that they are perfectly capable of doing when necessary ... but not deny their very nature. Of course, some women are naturally more competitive and assertive, like many men. We're all unique. Above all, it is important to be yourself and bring all you've got to your job. But to be effective in business, you may have to do some professional development work to play to your strengths and minimize what some may see as weaknesses, e.g., a squeaky voice.

When it comes to success, here is an important point to consider: Women don't need to mimic the old male model. They need not be afraid to step out and demonstrate their full capabilities. They can work on developing a style that uses and reflects their full spectrum of intelligence, a mix of linear analytical "masculine" skills with intuitive nurturing "feminine" (people) skills. Once women learn how to do this, they will be unstoppable in their careers.

And some women seem to be doing just that—bringing the best of their masculine and feminine skills into their jobs. Although I have not met any of today's high-profile female CEOs, such as Mary Barra, Marissa Mayer, Meg Whitman, or Ginni Rometty, they appear much more feminine to me than some of the previous high-profile businesswomen. They present a feminine yet professional image in the way they dress. The way they speak in interviews comes across as practical and down-to-earth. They appear approachable, and they seem to have maintained a sense of humility.

Another business leader I applaud is Sheryl Sandberg. She appeared on a series of talk shows in 2017 to speak about her new book, *Option B*, and the tragic loss of her husband. While speaking, Ms. Sandberg allowed her painful, grief-stricken emotions to surface and be viewed. She said she wanted to share her difficult experience so that others might be helped.

It's time for certain behaviors traditionally viewed as negative in women to be accepted in business settings. Being emotional under certain circumstances, as Ms. Sandberg said she was at work after her husband's death, should be acceptable. Showing empathy, even toward competitors, can be effective. Hesitation can be beneficial. What may appear as indecisiveness in a situation may actually be the very thing needed—someone who is taking the appropriate time to weigh a myriad of facts in order to make a wise decision based on those facts. In our rapidly changing world, it is difficult for anyone to unequivocally set a direction without any mid-course adjustment. But we've all heard the clichés about women changing their mind. Instead, I am suggesting that characteristics and behaviors traditionally viewed as negative actually have positive potential; with this awareness comes a shift toward "feminine" attributes being perceived in a positive instead of a negative light.

Of course, it would be a mistake if we swung too far from the masculine model to adopt a strictly feminine model—a model where feelings and instincts took the place of facts and statistics. The traditional skills of both sexes are needed. A man or woman who is able to demonstrate both masculine and feminine behaviors is a much more interesting, balanced, and capable individual.

In addition to education, I would advise women to spend time thinking about their demeanor and style, getting feedback on how they are perceived, and, if required, adjust their style accordingly. Unfortunately for me, it wasn't until I smacked up against the glass ceiling that I felt strong enough and comfortable enough to stand in my power and be myself.

I personally underwent a significant change in how I "styled myself" as my career progressed. For much of my career, I focused on developing and emphasizing my masculine abilities instead of my feminine qualities. I focused on developing skills of decision-making, organizing, planning, and giving orders, while deemphasizing my creativity, sensitivity, intuition, and nurturing abilities. It wasn't until I became comfortable with my progress in my career that I realized I was shortchanging myself and the companies where I worked by not tapping into my full potential. When I started approaching the higher levels of management, I made a definite change and embraced the yin and yang in myself.

The career of Christa Quarles, who worked on Wall Street and became CEO of the restaurant-booking site OpenTable, Inc., reflects my own experience. Speaking of her career, Quarles says: "Early on, I suppressed my femininity. I suppressed what it meant to be a more nurturing individual. As I've aged, I've blended the two pieces together, recognizing I can be strong, I can be powerful, while still being humane and nurturing to the people around me. You play the rules of the game you're in. Once you get to the top of the game, you can change the rules."[17]

What I'd like to propose is that women change the rules before they reach the top ... that they demonstrate competence while maintaining their femininity.

EIGHT

Using Sexual Appeal in the Workplace

It was the early 1990s. In spite of feeling my career was progressing slowly, I was in fact moving up the corporate ladder into the senior levels of management. I was now viewed as the "right-hand man" of the CIO of United Airlines and believed I was being groomed to be his replacement.

Affirmative action guidelines were in place for most major companies, and the statistics of my company did not look good in terms of advancing women and minorities. Although there were many women employed in my company, few reached the higher ranks.

This was a period of minding my Ps and Qs. I didn't want to create enemies who might block my advancement in the future. I was more conservative in my approach to projects, avoiding the inherent risks of failure in promoting more creative ideas—an approach that may not have been the best for my company, but one I saw as the least likely to keep me from falling off the corporate ladder.

As a normal course of doing business, outside vendors were expected to present their products and services to me before approaching the CIO. At my first meeting with a particular software company that apparently hired only women for its sales force, I couldn't help but notice the many young, attractive women presenting their company's products. Although seeing attractive women in business was not unusual, what was unusual about these women was not only the way they dressed, wearing low-cut blouses and tight-fitting clothes, but their demeanor—it was anything but professional. Some of them brazenly flirted with the male customers in the meeting, leaning over them so that their breasts were clearly visible and acting far more provocative than anything I had ever witnessed in a workplace setting.

Many of the men in the meeting were much more attentive than usual, which only intensified the scorn I felt toward them and the saleswomen, and it must have shown on my face. *What pushovers these men are*, I said to myself. But I didn't say anything out loud. In part, I didn't have the nerve to voice what I was thinking. But mostly I didn't want an issue to be made of anything I might say during my period of careful behavior. Therefore, I endured the presentation and was noncommittal as to what my recommendation would be to the CIO.

After the meeting I did not recommend this company's products because of technical deficiencies in their software. Although I wondered whether the saleswomen's conduct had influenced my decision, I felt justified in my opinion. Shortly afterward, the CEO of the vendor company called my boss and tried to challenge my decision and discredit my judgment. My boss did not fall for the CEO's tactics. He invited me to join the call and supported my recommendation.

The fact that I did not endorse this company made no difference to its eventual phenomenal success. It continued to acquire other companies and became a dominant force in the software business. And it continued to use provocative women in its sales force strategy.

Looking back, I'm disappointed that I did not confront the issue of the saleswomen's conduct. By not voicing any objection, I, in effect, endorsed their excessively provocative behavior. Even worse, I have to admit that although I wasn't as blatant in my use of sex appeal as these saleswomen were, I had done my own fair share of subtly using my sexuality to get attention through my dress and actions. I found it easy to dress provocatively, perhaps wearing a pair of suit pants that were just a little too tight (as often happened when I gained a few pounds from my husband's good cooking). And I knew there were times when I walked past a group of men a bit too slowly in my tight-fitting pants. So how could I fault these women, who simply had the courage to be more forward than me? I felt somewhat hypocritical, knowing I had merely used subtler forms of allurement than those women.

Eventually, the CEO of the software firm who had used women so blatantly in his sales force was indicted for other reasons, strengthening my belief that once a company demonstrates less than ethical practices in one area, other wayward practices are more easily adopted by the corporate culture.

○ ○ ○ ○

A few years later, I was surprised when women's camisole-style tops with bra straps and lace around the bodice came into vogue and were worn by many businesswomen under their suit jackets. My mom said I was being prudish (and she may have been right), but in my opinion these tops looked more appropriate for the bedroom than the boardroom. Are we women just seeing how far we can go to be titillating to the men at work? I wondered.

Let's face it ... many of us women are used to playing the seductive role. It's second nature to us. But what is our message when we wear such attire? Are we signaling that we can damn well wear what we please, and no one can tell us what to do or what to wear? And if anyone dares to make a comment about our attractiveness, we'll sue you.

The use of sexuality is a common way for women to feel powerful. Oftentimes, using sex appeal is the only time that a woman feels powerful. From my personal experience, I felt powerful when a man was attracted to me. He may not have been interested in my business opinion, but he wanted my attention and favor—at least for the moment. I could reward him or withhold my attention. The choice was mine ... not his. This in turn may have left him feeling less empowered, though at that point, I don't think he cared too much about power. The problem with using sexuality in the workplace is that it keeps a woman locked in a stereotypical role and does not truly empower her. On the contrary, it ultimately erodes her self-esteem, as she wonders whether she is valued for anything other than her sexual appeal. If she manages to succeed, will everyone assume she had been "sleeping her way to the top"?

Looking back on my career, I wish I had placed less emphasis on my looks and attire, and not used flirting and my sexuality to my advantage—not because of how I impacted men, but because I had less confidence that my performance was the primary reason I was recognized and promoted. Were other, less attractive women better leaders and business people than I was? I wondered at the time. Were they overlooked because they did not use their sexuality? Furthermore, using my sexuality never left me feeling empowered for very long.

As my career progressed, I became very conscious of how my appearance and dress could be viewed—these physical externalities that women must take so seriously but men don't have to worry about very much. I decided that although some men will fall for seductive ways, others will not, and may criticize or dismiss a woman because of the way she dresses or acts. I also came to realize that many other professional women might react the same way I did toward the provocative saleswomen and not be inclined to support someone who dresses or acts provocatively.

I have always loved fashion, and had been one of the first to adopt new styles since my teens. I took full advantage of casual Fridays to don the latest look at work. If I was in the workplace today, I know it would be difficult for me to resist the current trend of feminine tulle skirts paired with combat boots. For me, that represents the feminine and masculine, the yin and the yang, the dance floor and the hiking trails. That said, I am not recommending women adopt this look for work.

o o o o

Another big topic related to sex in the workplace is the issue of having affairs with colleagues. Meeting people at work and dating them is understandable, and it's practical, particularly because people spend so many of their waking hours at work. As with the use of sex appeal, however, it would be naïve for a woman to think that her office affair won't be noticed by bosses and peers.

In the interest of full disclosure, I must admit that I had several romantic involvements with colleagues and superiors (one that I sorely regret). Fortunately, these affairs were in the earlier part of my career, when I was in lower-level positions. As I attained higher levels of management, I became more image conscious. And once I was married, I had no interest in love affairs.

Throughout my career, I frequently heard about affairs between men and women, even occurring at the most senior levels of companies. Whereas the men's reputations were generally not tarnished, the women were usually looked upon unfavorably. Perhaps this double standard is not fair, but it's a workplace reality that women must seriously consider.

I decided that if a woman is serious about attaining senior-level positions, she would do well to leave her romantic inclinations at home and avoid such entanglements at work. This applies to same-sex couples as well. Although office affairs are understandable, they are fodder for the gossip-mongers, and consequences, including loss of a job, can occur.

○ ○ ○ ○

While I don't advocate that women use sex appeal to gain promotions or other advantages in the workplace, I do recommend that women work on developing a positive body image. Since some of my self-esteem was tied to my appearance, I spent well over an hour every day on hair and makeup chores. Even after I married, I maintained these laborious routines. It wasn't until I was in my mid-seventies, when the Covid-19 pandemic forced me into lockdown, that I became less religious about my daily routines. What I have noticed is that without makeup, I look more like myself … more like Donna. Therefore, I have concluded that makeup not only helps me look and feel better, it also helps me to stay less visible, almost as if I am placing a mask over my face—a physical barrier to avoid showing my real self to the world.

Many women today alter their appearance with such enhancements as hair extensions, fake eyelashes, and Botox, not to mention hours with a personal trainer or surgical procedures. While costly, these interventions can save time and augment a woman's appearance to fit the ideal of the day. Yet, no matter how many body and facial enhancements a woman receives, I don't know one woman of any age—not one—who is totally satisfied with her appearance. Most women find something about their body they wish was different: weight, complexion, etc. I believe this attitude reduces most women's confidence ... and confidence is a critical success factor in any business.

Appearances become more of a liability as we age, because wrinkles are not viewed positively by most men or women. Aging can be even more challenging for those of us who have used appearances to our advantage, as I certainly did and now have to reconcile my aging body with my former self-image.

Young women today face new challenges. Studies have shown that Instagram, Facebook's photo-sharing app, can be particularly harmful to teenage girls.[18] The research finds an alarming number of them spiraling toward eating disorders, depression, and unhealthy body images, when they see other girls online who more closely mirror a beauty ideal. Such toxic mindsets will bring another group of women into the workforce with inferior views about themselves.

The pressure for women to conform to standards of beauty was already ever-present in my younger years, as we flipped through fashion magazines or viewed ads on television. Today, with social media, the barrage of idealized images is ubiquitous, relentless, and constant. How sad that we women have been so superficially conditioned. I am not against beauty-enhancing techniques; but I am against tying physical appearance to self-esteem and confidence. The key, as always, is balance. By all means, pay attention to your grooming and enjoy your wardrobe. But I encourage all women who are building a career to resist feeling obligated to adopt a media-approved image of female attractiveness.

NINE

The Unique Challenge of Meetings

Business meetings can be challenging for everyone involved. But if you are a woman, the challenges become exponentially more difficult. The power dynamics of business meetings are interesting to watch. An entire book could be written about the subject—where to sit, when to speak, how to speak, when not to speak, whom to sit next to.... Being confined to an enclosed room with others, where tensions are prone to running high, can be uncomfortable, even daunting—especially for more sensitive, less extroverted people. It took years of practice for me to find a level of comfort at meetings that were predominantly male-dominated.

I felt more comfortable in one-on-one conversations or in small groups than in large meetings. In addition, men seemed to be more open and willing to negotiate with me privately, probably because they didn't have any turf to protect, face to save, or reputation to uphold.

Mandatory attendance in meetings was a daily occurrence for me, however. If a meeting was an important one, the room would be occupied almost exclusively by men—at times, entirely by men—except for myself and the occasional note-taking assistant. In contrast, whenever a meeting was not viewed as critical to the ongoing viability of the company, more women would be present. While white women today attend more high-level meetings, women of color sometimes find themselves to be both the only woman and the only person of their race in meetings.

My nerves usually felt taut before an important meeting, as I knew my reputation could be enhanced or ruined by whatever I said. So seeing men act nervous and fidgety before a meeting, I could understand their desire to lessen their anxiety by chatting in small groups. As the men mingled and casually talked in groups of two or three, I would sometimes feel left out. Generally, I would approach a small group of men and try to join the conversation. Sometimes I felt welcomed; more often, however, I felt like an intruder.

○ ○ ○ ○

When I was in high school, there was one girl in my class who was by far the most unpopular. Her clothes and hairdo were out of style, and she was a little bigger and stockier than most of us. She often sat alone in our lunchroom. Most students treated her as if she were invisible. Occasionally I would ask her to join my group of friends. Unfortunately, my friends tended to ignore her, but she didn't seem to notice their rebuff—at least, she didn't act as if she was bothered.

Sometimes I felt like that unpopular classmate, especially before and during meetings. This exclusion was a new, discomfiting feeling for me, as I had always been popular. Even when one man tried to include me in an informal conversation, I didn't always feel welcomed by the group. And when that happened, I behaved similarly to the unpopular girl in my class ... as if I didn't notice that I was being ignored.

Something else I noticed in important meetings, and have heard other women mention as well, was the lack of eye contact I received from men. At first I thought that perhaps the men avoided looking at me for fear of having sexual thoughts, as my friend Cary had always maintained. But I wondered if they didn't want to look at me because they resented having a woman in the room. Or perhaps they thought I wouldn't be influential in the meeting, so why should they acknowledge my presence?

Whatever the reason, these subtle slights can be disarming. What made me most angry, however, was something that happened to me frequently—not being acknowledged for my input. On one such occasion, the senior officers in my company were meeting to discuss the company's continuing low marks on customer surveys. After being given somewhat of a cold shoulder before the meeting, I took a seat in the middle of the boardroom's long oval table, between two men who had always been cordial to me.

The meeting began with the president providing an overview of the company's dismal results in terms of customer satisfaction. The most recent survey indicated that too frequently our employees demonstrated poor attitudes and were not willing to go out of their way to help customers. Training and incentive programs had been put in place, but so far, nothing had improved customer satisfaction. After several comments had been made, I spoke up, believing I understood the source of the employees' morale problem, even though I felt it should have been obvious to everyone.

"I don't think the employees believe that we support them or understand them or value them," I began. "In order for customer service to improve, our employees must feel valued and be empowered to make decisions. So far, all of our efforts have been driven by our own ideas. Why don't we ask the employees how we can improve customer service? I'm sure they will have some good suggestions. Employee morale might even improve if we just listen to them and adopt some of their ideas."

"I think the problem is the customers' expectations," another vice president said in a loud voice, after I had barely finished talking. "We have trained the customer to expect too much service. We need to retrain our customers."

What an idiotic comment, I thought. Although in my opinion his suggestion smacked of arrogance, much discussion ensued. Other ideas were offered. Some received support, and others did not.

Then the president spoke up. "I think we should ask the employees for their ideas," he said. "I think they would feel valued if we ask them."

I sat up straight and folded my arms on the table in front of me. I couldn't believe what I had heard. I thought someone would surely speak up on my behalf and say that's what I had suggested earlier in the meeting. *Didn't they even hear me?* I wondered. *Am I invisible?*

Invisible—that's how I felt in this situation and how I often felt in meetings. I could not believe that no one in the room mentioned that the president's idea was identical to mine. If I had made only a brief comment, perhaps I could understand why my suggestion had been overlooked. But I had done a fairly thorough job of explaining my thoughts.

I believed the president to be an honest and fair man, so I thought perhaps he had been distracted and not heard me speak. Even though my voice was not as loud as most of the men's voices, that was not an issue here, as the boardroom's acoustics were good. I wondered if the other executives were afraid of offending the president if they supported me. Perhaps no one wanted to risk telling him that he hadn't been listening when I suggested the idea earlier; that a woman, no less, had already come up with this solution.

I was thoroughly irritated. I had experienced this way of being overlooked by my male colleagues so many times that I probably shouldn't have been surprised, but the slight continued to bother me. For a brief moment, I began doubting myself again, wondering if my communication skills were inferior. Could that have been the reason my idea wasn't acknowledged? I asked myself.

In hindsight, I should have spoken up for myself and said that I had previously mentioned the same idea. Of course, that would have been an affront to the president and a subtle indictment of all the men who had not stood up for me. Better, I could have graciously thanked the president for endorsing my idea, saying something like, "Thank you, Mr. President, for seconding the suggestion I made a few minutes ago."

Instead, I was upset and remained silent in the discussion that followed about how to obtain the employees' feedback. On one hand, I was glad the officers had agreed upon an approach that could make a positive difference to the company if it was carried out effectively; on the other hand, I felt hurt that my input had been ignored. Although lack of respect for men's input happens too, it is much more likely to happen to women.

My response at this particular meeting is a good example of the negative emotions and ensuing paralysis that discrimination of any kind evoked in me. Whenever I was ignored in some way, I felt disrespected. Then a cascade of other emotions quickly followed: First, I felt I must be inferior or lacking in some skill that caused me to be ignored; then I grew angry, because even if there was something wrong with me, common courtesy would be to acknowledge my remarks. So now I would be dealing with feelings of inferiority and anger, neither of which is productive.

I think my reactions were typical of someone who is discriminated against, whether that person is a female or another minority. Although some employees manage to regain their confidence and work through their anger, others hold onto negative emotions until they become destructive toward themselves or become less productive at the company. Some employees even shut down and no longer care about the future of the company. Executives should think about these negative consequences when employees are ignored or disrespected.

o o o o

Who supports whom in meetings can be as interesting to watch as the actual unfolding of the discussion. Another problematic situation that I often saw at meetings occurred later, when a group of managers met to discuss implementation of the president's directive to elicit employee involvement.

The meeting began with a suggestion from a HR manager. "Why don't we ask each manager in the company to have a meeting with their employees to solicit their input?" she suggested.

"That's a wonderful idea," another female HR manager said immediately (and a bit too exuberantly), obviously trying to be supportive of the first HR manager's suggestion.

What bothered me was the immediate support the HR manager gave her colleague, most likely because she was a woman. I often found that whether people supported or undermined each other, gender, race, or other biases were often at play.

○ ○ ○ ○

Perhaps as a result of being frequently ignored in meetings, many women I knew started talking in loud, commanding voices, essentially emulating how men talked. I could understand this reaction to being ignored, but I didn't think adopting the unyielding, dictatorial style of many male executives was the best solution for women. Although such aggressive styles may come across as strong and authoritative and get results, my experience was that men who projected an inclusive, welcoming tone in meetings were generally more effective in soliciting input and producing results. Furthermore, this inclusive, collaborative style of facilitation is a natural strength of many women.

Learning how to speak effectively to be heard and acknowledged in meetings is a skill I wished I had focused on. I believe it is a skill that becomes more important as a woman reaches higher positions of authority. Although I became much more comfortable speaking to large groups of employees and customers, I never became totally comfortable in male-dominated, internal meetings. Over time, I became more assertive with my comments in meetings, because I felt I had been ignored on so many prior occasions. Though I did not get as loud and aggressive as some women I knew, I became determined to be heard. But I never felt totally acknowledged, especially in a room full of men.

I often asked myself when my self-confidence began to diminish ... when did I start feeling that I wasn't on top of my game? I don't believe it was the intimidation and bullying that I encountered, or the failure to receive deserved promotions, or the sexual innuendos I received. I think it was those damn meetings with high-level male executives. For me, it was extremely disempowering to sit in those meetings and be ignored and dismissed. I eventually fought back against most of the other discriminatory treatment I received in one way or another; I asked for the promotions and equal salary (even though I may not have received them). But I didn't have the courage to call out a room full of men on their gross, rude, condescending behavior. Because I didn't do so, I lost confidence and respect for myself, which in turn made me more ineffective in meetings.

I grant you that calling out a roomful of men is extremely difficult for a woman to do, but it is something in hindsight that I wish I had done. Rather than condemning the men for their behavior in that meeting when my input was ignored, for example, I could have also stated how I was feeling … saying something such as: "I feel like my ideas are not being heard; let me reiterate my position." Even though I overcame my fear of public speaking for the most part, and grew comfortable in speeches in front of employees and customers, I could not gain that level of confidence with a room full of male executives.

○ ○ ○ ○

I remember the first time I was asked to speak at a conference held annually for representatives of the many travel agencies throughout the country. When I walked into the conference hall to rehearse my speech, workers were in the process of removing a partition in the middle of the hall. I felt frightened when I realized how big the hall would be and how many people would fill that space. I remember thinking *I can't do this*, but I knew it was too late to back out. Fortunately, I had a female colleague and friend who helped to calm me.

For the first time in my life, I had had a wardrobe expert put together my outfit for the event. She had chosen a mid-calf, loose-fitting plaid skirt, a crisp white blouse, a fitted navy-blue vest, and penny loafers. I hated it. The entire outfit was so different from my sexy Diane von Furstenberg dresses and high-heeled shoes. In my mind I looked like a throwback from the 1950s. My nervousness about the event had caused me to put faith in someone I considered to be an expert on business attire, rather than rely on my own sense of fashion.

Given my fashion sense, I'm surprised I was able to put aside my discomfort about my outfit during my speech. I had decided not to make my speech overly technical, as had been the tradition for many years. Instead, I made the speech entertaining and easily understood by the audience. After I finished, I had a hard time walking out of the hall because of all the people stopping me to offer congratulations. That was the last time, however, I allowed someone else to decide what I wore.

○ ○ ○ ○

I have always been an extremely sensitive person. While my sensitivity enables me to understand nuances and undertones that many people miss, I also pick up negative feelings and vibes from those around me. In the case of employees and customers, I felt most of them liked me, and those feelings made me feel accepted and gave me encouragement during my speeches. With high-level male executives, I often felt resentment, boredom, and condescension. I could not shake those feelings enough to be comfortable speaking in male-dominated meetings, even though I knew several men supported me. Women who have sensitive natures need to accept the fact that there will be men who resent their presence—perhaps even more so today, as women assume high-level positions. Practicing staying centered and confident in the face of negativity and disapproval can help women be effective and avoid growing defensive. I wish I had practiced such mind conditioning.

While there may be many reasons for women to lose self-confidence, it is most important to be aware when it is happening and to do something about it. If I was in the workforce today, I would sit down at least monthly and ask myself how I am feeling—powerful, confident, fulfilled, and growing—or timid, fearful, insecure, and stagnating? If my answer was the latter, I would take action—training, counseling, peer review, self-help books—to address how I felt. Actually, this is a good practice for any situation and stage in life.

TEN

Recognition

While most of my assignments had been technical in nature, in the early 1990s I was asked by senior management at United Airlines to work with outside consultants to streamline work activities in the company. I and one of my male colleagues were the primary internal leaders of the effort for the Information Technology (IT) division.

Although my colleague and I felt honored to be selected to lead the effort, we also had some misgivings and trepidation. The effort, called Introspect, involved going into all the departments in the division and recommending that some of their work be eliminated because it was redundant or non-critical. After the review, the personnel associated with these tasks would be laid off or reassigned—in effect saving the salary expense for those employees whose jobs were eliminated.

One can imagine this effort was not welcomed by most of the managers and employees in the division. Who wants to be told that their job is redundant or unnecessary, and therefore it and you may be eliminated? In addition to facing much internal resistance, my colleague and I resisted the efforts of the outside consultants to please senior management by inappropriately cutting work, thereby saving as much money as possible.

This highly political (and often unpleasant) effort continued for more than a year and did what it was designed to do: cut costs. What I didn't acknowledge at the time was that it was assumed I had these innate negotiating skills because I was a woman. Moreover, I didn't consider asking for additional pay for these skills. While I'm glad that progressive companies today are finally compensating women for their collaborative and negotiating skills, in addition to their technical and analytical skills, more women should demand payment for these skills.

○ ○ ○ ○

In my regular job as a Director of Applications Development for many of United's computer systems, I had a large budget. One day, several of my employees presented me with an idea about eliminating paper airline tickets. At the time this was revolutionary thinking, because the notion of a paperless environment had not been considered in most industries and certainly not in the airline industry.

After the employees developed a business plan for their idea, I took their proposal through the normal budgetary approval process. It was rejected on the grounds that customers would not acclimate to a paperless environment and would insist on having a paper ticket. I disagreed with the decision, but knew it would be an uphill battle to get corporate approval to proceed.

My next action could be seen as highly controversial. Having hundreds of employees working for me and extensive capital funds, I simply asked some of my department heads if they could get some of their work accomplished in a little less time and with a little less money. They were happy to oblige. That gave me the time and money to develop an electronic ticketing system, while still making our deadlines for other committed work. Some may call this action insubordination—I call it taking a risk and trying to do something beneficial for your company.

When the system was completed, we installed it as a pilot in a few airports. We called the system E-Ticket™. It was quickly accepted by travelers, particularly by some of our frequent flyers. The next challenge was to convince other airlines that E-Ticket™ was a good idea, so that customers could fly on multiple airlines without having a paper ticket. Fortunately, many other airlines saw the value of paperless ticketing.

United's E-Ticket™ system went on to be nominated that year as one of the top five technology endeavors in the U.S. It became part of the Smithsonian Permanent Research Collection on Information Technology at the National Museum of American History. Although United did not win the first place award that year (Carly Fiorina from Hewlett-Packard received that award), I proudly represented E-Ticket™ at the gala awards event in Washington.

In addition, I was able to eventually sell the E-Ticket™ software to fourteen other airlines and gain many millions of dollars for my company. Of note is that in spite of my external recognition, I never felt fully recognized internally by the senior executives in my company. Some colleagues called me the "Mother of E-Ticket™." Most had no idea of the risk I took in undertaking the development of the software.

∘ ∘ ∘ ∘

In 1994 I was named Woman of the Year of United Airlines for the annual YWCA's recognition event in New York. It was a great honor and thrill for me. I could bring one guest to the ceremony in New York, which would honor the year's nominees. My husband was not able to attend, so I invited my mom. It was one of the highlights of my career—to take Mom to New York, stay in a fancy hotel, and take in a play after the recognition event.

I remember how proud I felt as I stood on the stage in New York and heard my name announced. I was wearing a new business suit and watched Mom clapping enthusiastically in the audience. Then I marched back across the stage to the upbeat music and words of a Matthew Wilders song: "Ain't nothin' gonna break my style." I will never forget that song and those words. I bought the CD and played it over and over again for years, reliving that moment.

I also remember feeling excitement from some of the women in my company who attended the ceremony, and irritation from some of the men who were there. Perhaps the latter was just conjecture on my part, but they sure looked bored and unhappy. What is not conjecture, however, is that United Airlines dropped out of the program the next year. Regardless, the recognition made me feel more confident in my abilities and less cautious about watching my P's and Q's.

o o o o

Later that year I was named acting CIO for United Airlines. Though I had been hoping to receive the job for a long time, I was shocked when it happened … in effect being acknowledged and given entrance into the good-old-boys' club. For a woman to receive such a position at the time—to be CIO of a Fortune 100 company and given responsibility for the technology that was critical for most company functions, including flight planning and monitoring—was almost unheard of.

I didn't fully celebrate my achievement back then. Perhaps it was because I believed that my promotion was primarily due to one man, who was definitely not one of the good old boys. He was, however, very influential in decisions about who did or did not get promoted in the company and was a longtime supporter of me. He and I had worked closely together on a previous project, laughing and poking fun at the many dysfunctional situations we encountered. I adored that man and could hardly look at him without smiling. And oh, the stories he told me, including one about driving a top executive to his mistress's home during lunch hour.

The appointment as CIO gave me an instant boost of confidence. My hope was that once I proved myself in the acting CIO role, I would be awarded the permanent CIO position. Even though I was initially surprised by the promotion, I never once questioned whether I could do the job, and not only do the job, but do it better than my male colleagues. This was not because I believed I was smarter than most of my colleagues, or that my technology expertise was superior; it was because I believed I possessed the leadership skills to direct my two thousand employees to accomplish amazing results. Motivating employees was one of my strengths.

My attitude about leadership was different from most of the other executives I knew at the time. Most male executives seemed to believe that they had the position because of their superior knowledge, while I believed that I could produce better results by collaborating with my employees and supporting their ideas. Although I accepted that it was my responsibility to make high-level decisions, I firmly believed in a collaborative approach. I still do. Unfortunately, I think my lack of bravado and cockiness was seen as a deficiency.

Even though I had all the responsibility of a CIO of a Fortune 100 company, I did not receive the full recognition or pay associated with such a position, due to my "acting" title. Many people would regard this move up the ranks as progress because, unlike earlier in my career, I at least had the title, albeit with the word "acting" in front of it.

○ ○ ○ ○

Having worked in the division previously, I knew that the employees were not clear about their goals and objectives. Furthermore, the departments within the division did not work well together, just as the divisions throughout the company didn't work well together. It was obvious to me that team building and goal setting were needed. I knew it would be a major undertaking to get the employees in the division working better together. Although team building was not an idea that was popular in the company at the time, I believed it was critical to the success of work efforts.

Consequently, I led all of my more than two thousand employees through a series of facilitated roundtable discussions in which everyone had an opportunity to participate in setting the goals and objectives. The effort took many months, and I was proud of our accomplishment. Some employees may not have agreed with the goals that were established, but everyone was clear on what the goals were and knew that they were expected to work together to accomplish them. Then I hired some outside consultants to facilitate team-building exercises to ensure the success of the goals.

I also conducted events to bolster the morale of managers and employees in the division—holding award events for many who had never been recognized. Years earlier, I had attended a class at one of Walt Disney's theme parks in Florida to try to understand their company's culture, which excelled at customer service and employee appreciation. I was later chastised by a boss for attending the class, because that kind of culture was viewed as unprofitable. I took some of the concepts from that class, however, to empower and boost my employees' morale. I also used some of the experience I had gained by dancing and acting in musicals in high school and college to put on entertaining business events. I believed people can learn better through being entertained rather than being lectured to. Again, I knew these events were fodder for scorn and dismissal by most in upper management.

So often in my career, I felt my instincts were "right on" for the situation at hand, yet opposed to traditions and the ways of the good-old-boys' club. My biggest regret is that I often allowed myself to feel less than triumphant and positive about my accomplishments. Instead of reacting to sidelong glances, I should have been dancing with joy. Come on … the Smithsonian, for god's sake, and CIO of a Fortune 100 company! My fervent hope is that women today recognize and celebrate their strengths and successes. Do not let the good old boys diminish you.

While I was confident that I could do the CIO job well, it was a difficult time for me personally. In addition to the normal stresses for any CIO running the technology department of a major airline, my father had been hospitalized in another state. I flew to be by his bedside every other weekend, primarily to confront his doctors over his treatment, which I considered inadequate. He had lapsed into a coma-like state before hearing that I had become a CIO.

Yet, in spite of my stress level, I felt I was doing a good job. I think one of the most hurtful things that ever happened to me in my career was that after my father's death, not one of the good old boys offered his condolence. Perhaps they didn't know. If so, it was just one more sign of how excluded I was from their club.

○ ○ ○ ○

Within a year of acting as CIO for United Airlines, a new top management team took over the company. I documented the team-building process I had undertaken in a memo to the new president, who had said in his first presentation to his executive team that teamwork was very important to him.

Although I tried not to get my hopes up too high, I couldn't help but feel expectant about getting the permanent CIO position. The computer systems were running smoothly; many long-standing problems identified by the user community had been solved; I had the support of my employees; and I had focused on the very thing the new president had said was important to him—teamwork.

ELEVEN

Smacking Up Against the Glass Ceiling

When I had my first opportunity to spend some time alone with the new president of United Airlines, he immediately told me that I was not being considered for the permanent CIO job; they would be conducting a search to find someone outside of the company. I felt devastated. That left me as an acting CIO, without the permanent title or associated pay, and the distinct feeling that I was not being given credit for my greatest accomplishments.

I was angry about the president's quick dismissal of me. He seemed to have little interest in hearing about one of the very things he said was most important to him—teamwork. He obviously knew nothing about me and my work, other than what he had been told by the other, mostly male, officers. Even more infuriating, I knew I was doing an exceptional job. Maybe I didn't swagger around the office boasting about my accomplishments, but damn it, the work was getting accomplished with fewer problems than in the past. Despite my extreme frustration and disappointment, I felt that I needed to be professional, so I pretended that I wasn't feeling hurt and just carried on with my responsibilities.

I see the way I handled not receiving the permanent CIO position as one of the biggest failures of my career. I allowed my feelings of hurt and anger to thwart steps I should have taken on my own behalf. I meekly accepted the defeat with no pushback. Taking action may not have changed the outcome (being given the permanent CIO position), but I would have felt better if I had made a strong case to the president and the new executive team about my qualifications. Instead, I accepted the defeat without any resistance.

Several months later I was invited to attend a three-day conference with the senior officers of the company. Although I knew I would feel like an outcast because of my "acting" title, I also knew many of the men were also apprehensive about the offsite event. All we had been told was that we would be going into the wilderness for three days of team building.

○ ○ ○ ○

The offsite event began with a dinner. After dinner most everyone went into a bar for a nightcap before retiring. On one side of the bar was a small room reserved for cigar smoking, into which most of the senior officers soon disappeared. Before long, those of us remaining seated at the bar could see—and smell—clouds of smoke billowing from the room.

How horrible it would be to be in that room, I thought. Although I certainly wasn't expected to join the men in the room, since I didn't have a senior officer title, I wondered what I might have done if I had held the permanent CIO position. What made the situation even more irritating to me was that the conference was supposed to be a team-building event. If there ever was a way to discourage team building, hiding in a smoke-filled room was surely a good start. I wondered if the conference leaders, who were outside consultants hired by the company, saw the irony in the situation.

Most troubling about this situation was that I felt I would never fit in with the senior officers. Aside from the obvious—being a woman—I was just too different. My interests weren't the same as theirs. I didn't enjoy talking about the same things. For sure, I didn't enjoy smoking cigars. I realized that some men felt the same way I did, of course—like my friend George, who would have been uncomfortable in this kind of macho setting. Unfortunately for me, he had dropped out of the corporate world because he didn't think he fit into the old boys' club either.

The evening reminded me of so many times in my career when I had felt that no matter what I did to prove myself, I would never be accepted or adequately recognized. Times had now changed in the corporate world—at least to the extent that women were being included in golf and other sports outings; though few women could compete with men in these physical endeavors.

How much do I want to change to fit in? I asked myself on countless occasions. I didn't want to accept the fact that it might never happen. This conference event brought this issue to the forefront of my mind. I went to my room that night feeling excluded and lonely.

○ ○ ○ ○

My discomfort only became worse when the team-building events began the next day. We were separated into teams of ten individuals. The first event required traversing a maze of trees by swinging on ropes. I knew I wouldn't be able to perform that exercise well, because I didn't have the upper-body strength.

As I stood on the sidelines, a conference leader approached me. "That's all right, Donna," he said. "There will be other events you can participate in."

The next exercise involved a rope-pulling contest. Now, who would want a 105-pound weakling like me on their team? Clearly the "team-building" event had not been designed to include everyone on the team.

Although I did my best to perform all the exercises, I usually felt at a disadvantage because of my height and weight. I tried to participate wholeheartedly in the conversations and critiques that preceded and followed the physical exercises, but I was feeling so inadequate that I found it difficult to join in with confidence. I wondered if the smaller men and other women felt as out of place as I did.

That night I saw one of the top females in the company leave the dining room with tears in her eyes. I suspected she was having difficulty handling the conference as well. Like Faye, she had always projected a strong, aloof facade.

I felt particularly upset because I believed I had already demonstrated the very skills this conference was trying to teach these officers—team building—and my work as acting CIO had been ignored or gone unnoticed. The president had finally followed up on my invitation to review the results of the team-building efforts in my division. Although I felt he was just trying to appease me, he at least had the courtesy to listen to me.

As soon as the conference was over, the officers went back to their usual routine of backstabbing each other and protecting their turf. Honestly, I saw no sign of change in their behavior.

∘ ∘ ∘ ∘

No matter how many opportunities and successes I had in my career, I felt there was something missing at my core. I thought there was something wrong with me.

Of course there was something amiss with me. No matter how hard I tried, I would never, ever be one of the good old boys. And even though I knew that my conclusion that there was something wrong with me was incorrect, it was nonetheless damaging to my self-esteem.

From my earliest days, I always believed that if I was provided with a challenge, I could figure out a way to overcome that challenge. That attitude had served me well. I believe this attitude was the primary reason I was given one challenging assignment after another. My bosses and colleagues recognized this attribute. They had more faith in my abilities than I had in myself. Yet no matter how many successes I had, I was not able to heal that core belief that I was somehow lacking.

∘ ∘ ∘ ∘

The search for the new CIO took many months. During that time, the computer systems continued to run more smoothly than they had in many years. I could actually point to statistics to confirm that claim.

I believed this was in part due to my collaborative management style, coupled with the goal-setting and team-building sessions I had done with my employees.

As acting CIO, I gained invaluable experience running a worldwide technology organization. There were times when I thought I would have done the job for free, just to gain the experience. But I was well aware that once a new CIO was hired, I would have to make a decision whether to stay or to leave the company; I was fairly certain I would decide to leave.

∘ ∘ ∘ ∘

Surprisingly, Randy, the man brought into the company to become the new CIO, was someone I liked and respected from the first time we met. He understood my bruised feelings and seemed to want me to be a part of his organization. We became friends, and I helped him furnish his new estate with antiques.

In addition to my expertise in technology, I had extensive knowledge about antiques. I owned a four-story Victorian house that I had turned into an antiques business, which I used as an escape from the stresses and disappointments of the corporate world. I had even decorated my office at United with some pieces from my shop: a tall four-drawer file cabinet; a round oak table that I used for meetings; and various vintage pictures that added interest to the room. I knew of no other executive who had brought such unusual and unique furnishings to their office space. My antiques business—while on a much smaller scale than a large corporation—also gave me the experience of managing all facets of an entrepreneurial business.

Randy created a new organization for me to head up. Based on the E-Ticket™ success, the organization's mission would be to market and sell the company's other technologies. I couldn't have dreamed of a more perfect job that would enable me to use my technical and marketing skills; the organization would give me the opportunity to run my own little business with all the support and benefits from our parent company.

After not being given the permanent CIO position, I had thought I could never again be truly enthusiastic about a position in that company. I was wrong. After minimal consideration, I accepted the job. Furthermore, Randy had given my new position a vice-president title and officer status. At last I felt as if I were being appreciated and recognized.

When Randy sought approval for the new organization, however, he was not able to make me an officer of the company. I was quite disappointed, because I thought he had already gotten approval to make me an officer. The position, in my mind, clearly carried the responsibility to warrant the title, so I couldn't understand why it had not been approved, other than to think someone in HR or someone else didn't want me to be an officer. There was even another officer in the company—a man, of course—who had similar responsibilities.

I wasn't totally surprised that the head of HR didn't support me, because even though I had been fulfilling one of the major functions of the company during the past year, whenever he saw me or passed me in the hallways, he would not look at me directly or greet me. He seemed to intentionally avoid eye contact with me, which in turn made me feel very uncomfortable.

Even though I had made the difficult decision to stay with the company and believed I was perfect for the new job, here I was, once again, not being given the title or the pay that fit the position. As I sat with Randy in his office after he told me the bad news, I felt angry and extremely disappointed.

"Okay, Randy," I said. "I need to know the truth about what's going on with me. Why don't they think I should be an officer?"

"They just don't think the position warrants an officer ranking," Randy said.

"You know, and I know, that's not true. If the candidate was someone they thought should be an officer, we both know that's what would have happened. Why don't they think I should be an officer?"

Randy just stared at me and didn't say anything.

"C'mon, Randy. Tell me. I have a right to know."

"Some of the officers don't think you're strong enough. They think you're too weak."

"Weak!" I practically screamed at him. "After everything I've been through in my career? How can they possibly think I'm weak? They don't know the meaning of the word."

"I think they're absolutely wrong," Randy said, "but I think I'm too new in the company to fight them on their decision."

And then I began to cry. I felt certain that if the officers could have seen me then, they would have thought my tears validated their position.

Randy moved the Kleenex box on his desk closer to me.

"Now you think I'm weak too," I said, as I continued to cry. "I just can't take being put down anymore."

"I can understand how you feel right now, but don't make any rash decisions. Give yourself some time to think about what you want to do. Don't do something that you might regret later. At least get another job before you quit."

I knew Randy was giving me good advice. My husband had not been feeling well recently, and I was worried about what was going to happen to him. This would not be a good time to be out of work.

○ ○ ○ ○

The idea of being considered weak was something I had thought about a lot. I knew I was exceptionally strong. Mom had always said no one would ever break my will. I credited my strength to having wrestled with and conquered situations in my past, such as standing up to my father as a child, overcoming panic attacks without medication, and fighting my way successfully into male-dominated environments. But women who were sensitive and caring, as I also was, were automatically categorized as weak. Furthermore, I reflected that although I considered myself a strong person, my self-confidence had been eroded over the years, and at times I *did* feel weak. *How could it have been otherwise,* I thought to myself, *with the unfair treatment over the years in pay and title, being ignored in meetings, and other daily subtle putdowns?* Of course I came across as hesitant and weak at times. I abhorred bragging and bullying, and I felt beaten down.

I was aware that most of the officers had typecast me as being too much of a "people person," which at the time was equated with weakness. Businessmen were considered to be strong if they ignored the people element in making decisions, as long as they stayed within the law (or at least didn't get caught or have an uprising on their hands). The bottom line was all that mattered.

The fact is, I truly cared about my employees, and they, in turn, wanted to do an exceptional job to please me. I believed that my sincere concern for employees was the primary reason I obtained such high productivity levels. If an employee had a problem, I would stay after work as late as necessary to talk through the issue, even if the problem was something personal that was affecting his or her work.

I was not in sync with the corporate culture of the time. Years later, efforts would be made to improve company performance by treating employees better, but the old command-and-control style of management was still in vogue in that company, even though it was considered to be outdated by more progressive companies. At the time, my approach was considered frivolous. The team building and other employee events that I used to help motivate employees were viewed as unnecessary expenses that took time away from productive work. The factual productivity statistics I compiled and presented were viewed as biased or the result of other factors.

With regard to the question of strength versus weakness on the job, I actually viewed myself as tougher than most of my male colleagues. It all depends on one's definition of toughness. If toughness is defined as swaggering with your chest puffed out, pounding your fist in meetings, and speaking in a loud, authoritative voice, then I was not tough. If toughness is defined as taking a difficult stance and sticking to it; or refusing to do something unethical even if you might be fired; or taking disciplinary action with employees who were performing poorly, then I was truly strong.

For a long time, I had known that my definition of strength and the definition in vogue were polar opposites. My nickname was "Corporate Conscious." I could only wonder, didn't the officers realize how difficult it might be to take the stances that would earn such a title? Furthermore, why was I given one difficult, critical assignment after another? Were these the kind of assignments you give to your weak people?

Obviously, being told that I was viewed as weak made me furious, more furious than I had ever been. I can't even describe the frustration I felt. I was frustrated because feeling and acting like a female was holding me back. Showing emotions, especially crying, was considered to be a sign of weakness in women.

Shortly after being told that my new position would not hold an officer title, my husband and I returned home from a vacation to learn he was terminally ill. The thought of leaving the company and starting over in some other position was unthinkable to me at the time. Perhaps making the decision to stay was one of the biggest copouts of my career (as well as a demonstration of weakness), but I felt I needed the support of familiar colleagues and surroundings as I dealt with my husband's illness. And most important, I needed the company's medical insurance benefits for my husband.

○ ○ ○ ○

As I look back on my time as an acting CIO without the full title and pay, I understand much better what was going on. Times were changing. The fact that all the officers were expected to go to a team-building course was a far cry from the usual management class. It must have been intimidating for many of them, who had been raised on a command-and-control model, to suddenly have to listen to their employees and find ways to empower them. What an affront to their egos! And then there was this soft-spoken slight of a woman, who may have some talent and knowledge, but certainly lacked the kind of strength and ability necessary to run an important division. I did not fit the mold. On top of the changing management styles, most of the men must have felt equally threatened by the frequent change in top management and uncertain of their own survival in the company.

What I suspect happened to me and other women was we ran smack into the built-in bias against women being successful in the business world. When there are clear, quantifiable measurements for success (such as grades in school), women excel. But when the measurement becomes murkier or outside factors impact success (as happens in most businesses), women are held to a different—usually unfair—standard, even though they might be doing an excellent job. As an example, there was no possible way for customer service levels in Faye's department to remain high after she was forced to eliminate hundreds of employees!

Furthermore, every man and woman has some area in which improvement is needed—no one is perfect. Positive attributes and accomplishments can be focused on, or attention can be placed on negative ones. It often seemed to me that men got a pass, and women did not.

○ ○ ○ ○

I stayed on with United Airlines while my husband became progressively sicker and eventually died, two years after his diagnosis. Randy's support during this trying time was invaluable; he encouraged me to spend as much time as possible at my husband's bedside, which I did.

TWELVE

Compensation Disparity

Compensation was a topic that upset me during most of my career, and, not surprisingly, I eventually reached a boiling point. Throughout my career I had tried not to focus on wage inequities, because I usually became angry when I thought about the disparity between my pay and that of my male colleagues, and I thought that over time the inequity would be rectified when organizations such as HR were made aware of the injustice. What happens in practice, however, is that even though two individuals (perhaps a man and a woman) may be performing basically the same job, a case can usually be made in favor of the higher-paid individual possessing more education or experience, or doing something slightly differently than the other person.

Furthermore, many HR departments do not have the power to rectify wage inequalities; they are overridden by executives from departments that are viewed as more critical to the company. So rather than be upset most of the time, I believed that if I focused on developing my knowledge and skills, better pay would come with time … and it did, but never to the level of my male counterparts.

Even before I entered the business world in the 1970s, I had several experiences with unfair compensation. When I was in high school, I worked for an independent company that owned a drycleaner with an adjacent laundromat. Initially, I was just responsible for taking in and handing out the dry cleaning; next I was asked to clean the laundry machines and mop the floors each night; and then I was asked to do the bookkeeping for both parts of the business. I didn't receive higher pay for doing these additional tasks.

Another disturbing experience occurred in my job as a teacher after graduating from college. All of the teachers in my district were assigned extra duties in addition to their regular classes. My extra duty was to oversee a study hall of approximately two hundred junior-high students in the school's cafeteria. Another teacher, Mr. Ponch, had joint responsibility for monitoring the students with me.

Each week before the study hall began, I would watch Mr. Ponch walk to the back of the cafeteria, sit down in a chair, open his newspaper, and hold it in front of his face. Frequently, disruptions occurred when students shot wads of paper through peashooters or performed other disruptive antics. This was invariably followed by laughing and ballyhooing from other students. While I would try to quiet the students, Mr. Ponch kept his newspaper in front of his face, not bothering to even glance over to see what was happening; he couldn't have helped hearing the commotion.

Mr. Ponch's refusal to support me in managing the study hall infuriated me, and I felt his behavior demonstrated a lack of respect for me. Thus, the study hall session became the worst part of my week. I dreaded the effort required to keep the students quiet, and I didn't like the way I felt toward Mr. Ponch for not helping me.

Today I would be embarrassed by my failure to take issue with the disrespectful behavior of my colleague. But at the time I felt grateful to have a teaching job, and Mr. Ponch was a good friend and drinking buddy of our principal. Furthermore, at that stage in my life, I thought anger was an unacceptable emotion and did not know how to deal with it. Unfortunately, when anger that has been buried finally surfaces, it can be explosive.

One day Mr. Ponch was absent, and Maryla, my colleague who had taught me how to knit, came to the cafeteria to assist me with the study hall. She proactively helped me to settle down the students and keep them quiet.

"Thanks so much for helping me, Maryla," I said. "This is the first time anyone has really helped me."

"I thought Mr. Ponch was assigned to this study hall too."

"He is, but he doesn't do a thing but read his paper. He doesn't even look at the kids."

"That's unfortunate, because he's paid to watch over this study hall."

"What do you mean, he's paid?" I asked, the full impact of her statement not yet registering with me.

"Well, he has a family to support, so he's paid as if he was teaching an extra class."

I couldn't believe what she had said. Not only did this man not do his job, but he was being paid to not do his job.

If I had been a bull in the ring with a bullfighter, he should have run! Without saying a word to my colleague, I hurried out of the study hall, ran up the two flights of stairs to the first floor of the building, and marched past the secretary into the principal's office.

"What do you mean by paying Mr. Ponch and not me for the study hall?" I asked, breathing heavily with a reddened face and my hands on my hips.

"He has a family to support and you don't," the principal said calmly, as if he could have cared less that I was upset.

"That is totally unacceptable. I expect you to pay me the same as him. You don't have any idea what my personal needs are, and it is none of your business."

"All right, I'll think about it."

"You'd better do it, or I will talk to the board."

After leaving his office, I burst into tears of humiliation. How could I have been so stupid to do all the work and not get paid?

Although this type of unfairness was prohibited in later years, I believe from my own experience that this underlying attitude—that men should be better paid than women for the same work—continues to prevail in the business world. Obviously, the persistent wage gap between women and men bears this out.

○ ○ ○ ○

As I mentioned in an earlier chapter, after leaving my low-paying job as a teacher, I took a further pay cut when I joined the Big Eight accounting firm in the early 1970s. As I also mentioned, women at the time were paid less than 60% of what men earned. But since I was one of the first women hired into the consulting division, I felt honored to work there, and therefore didn't question my salary. Furthermore, the training that I was going to receive was worth as much to me as my salary, because I desperately wanted a management career—a career that was not an option for most women at the time.

I received excellent performance reviews and good pay increases as my career progressed. But even when I changed companies, my salary was much lower than that of my male counterparts for several reasons: First, companies usually base pay on one's previous salary, and it is difficult to catch up when starting out so far behind; second, my male counterparts were advancing more quickly in title and position.

In addition to the financial ramifications of not being paid the same as men, the psychological consequences can be significant as well; when a woman is paid less than her counterparts for similar work, she feels less valued and respected. At least that was the case for me, and I know I wasn't alone in feeling that way. Many of my female colleagues complained about their salaries, too.

As the years went by, my unfair pay continued to be a hot-button issue for me, always simmering under my surface. Although I never knew for sure how much less I was being paid than my male colleagues, I felt pretty certain that that was the case.

In the mid-nineties, when I became acting CIO, I finally had the opportunity to see all the salary figures of my colleagues, because they were now my subordinates. Prior to this, although I strongly suspected I was being paid less than my peers, I had not been privy to their exact salaries. Therefore, I was shocked when I realized that all of my male colleagues were being compensated substantially more than me.

At first I tried to rationalize the inequity by reasoning that several men had more seniority than I did, even though years of service were not relevant factors at our management levels. I figured that one of my subordinates, who was African American, had probably negotiated a high salary when he was recently hired. The company had few minorities in executive positions and was under pressure to hire and promote them. Yet as much as I tried to justify the difference between my pay and my subordinates' pay, I knew that my education, experience, and responsibilities far surpassed their credentials. No matter how I looked at it objectively, I knew that my job warranted a higher salary. But since I was hoping to become the permanent CIO, I decided to wait and insist that the injustice be rectified at the time of my anticipated promotion.

At the end of the year, I received a smaller increase than any of my subordinates. By that time, I knew I would not be getting the permanent CIO position and made an appointment with a man to whom I was temporarily reporting. I was determined to handle myself professionally, but I knew my anger was barely in check by the time I sat down in his office.

"I am extremely dissatisfied with the pay raise I received," I said, trying to remain calm. "You approved much higher increases for all of my direct reports, and they had higher salaries than I did before their raises. I don't think that's fair."

"I think your failure to successfully complete the project in Atlanta does not warrant a higher increase."

"What?" I almost shouted in disbelief. "Are you kidding? You were overseeing that project. It had problems for over four years, and I became involved only during the past several months, when it was too late to rescue it. Besides, that's only one of many projects I have been responsible for, most of which have been highly successful." I found it totally inconceivable he would try to lay any blame on me for my brief involvement in the failed Atlanta project.

"Anyway, it's too late to change the salary recommendations," he said. "All the input has been finalized."

"I'm sure HR will listen to you if you tell them to make an adjustment."

"I'll see what I can do," he said, looking irritated and abruptly ending the conversation.

Needless to say, my salary was not changed, even though I thought HR would have been glad to make an adjustment if he had requested it. I figured he just didn't want to be bothered with talking to HR on my behalf. I often wondered whether he and many of the top executives still believed that women should stay at home, as their wives did, and not take money away from the men.

o o o o

Later, during another annual pay-increase period, my boss had been out of town for quite a while. One day, as I was standing outside of a conference room, a colleague who had a lesser title and position than I did, handed me a form that was used to notate salary adjustments. I glanced briefly at the form, saw my small increase, and then tore both copies of the paper into pieces in front of him. My colleague looked at me in dismay. I regretted making him feel uncomfortable, but I knew my action would get back to our boss. It did. My colleague let our boss know that I had torn the papers to shreds, including the original form that needed to be turned into HR in order to make the salary adjustment effective.

The next time I saw my boss, I was standing in a hallway when he grabbed me firmly by the arm. No one else was around. Then he pulled me into an empty conference room, spun me around to face him, and slammed the door with his other hand.

"What do you mean by tearing up that paper?" he shouted.

"What do you mean by giving me such a paltry increase?" I yelled back at him. "I'm sick and tired of not being paid what I deserve. Do you understand the humiliation of having someone lower than me see how much I'm paid, when I'm paid so much less than the men at my level?"

The angry, accusatory insults went on from there.

As I look back on that confrontation, it's easy to see that years of suppressed anger had caught up with me.

Eventually I received some additional stock options when I continued to complain about my unfair salary, which ended up being worthless when the company went into bankruptcy.

∘ ∘ ∘ ∘

In hindsight, although I eventually fought for equal pay at different points in my career, I often bided my time before doing so. Early on in my career, I tried to find justifiable reasons for the lower pay, such as not having an MBA degree. So I went out and earned an MBA to level the playing field—but I was still paid less than my male colleagues.

Interestingly though, unless faced with gross disparity, I was reluctant to fight for myself … until I was ready to go ballistic. Could it be that I didn't think I deserved equal pay? Had I been conditioned into thinking that women should be paid less than men? Or was I just afraid of losing my job if I complained too much or made too many waves? I think the reason for my reluctance to address the wage issue was a combination of not wanting to be seen as a troublemaker, fearing the consequences if I pressed the issue, and disliking confrontation.

The reality is that when someone starts their career earning 60% less than their colleagues, it is very, very difficult to ever catch up with them. It's also important not to be misled into thinking a few cents here and there are not that important.

In March 2020, *Newsweek* reported that a typical woman in the U.S. will lose $407,760 over a forty-year career due to the gender wage gap.[19]

The loss for women of color is even greater, with black women losing $944,800 and Latina women losing $1,121,440. Most studies agree that it will be 2059 before U.S. women reach wage parity with men, and significantly longer for much of the world to catch up. Just think what a difference that extra money could make in a woman's life and retirement.

Due to the failure to close the pay gap, several cities and states are either in the process of evaluating or have passed laws to prohibit employers from basing wages of newly hired women on past history, which obviously hurts women who have been paid a lower wage than men.

For women starting their own business, funding has also been an issue. In an effort to understand the reason for women receiving lesser amounts of money than men, Columbia Business School doctoral candidate Dana Kanze found that "two-thirds of the questions asked of male entrepreneurs focused on the company's potential for success," while two-thirds of the female founders were asked questions about preventing the company's failure.[20]

If I were entering the workforce today, changing jobs, or up for a promotion in a company, I would use every avenue available to ascertain what a fair salary—one comparable to men in the same type of position—would be. If I were not offered a fair salary, I would use appropriate channels (HR, bosses, EEOC, etc.) to rectify the situation. If not rectified, I would look for another job. Of course, you might point out that this is easy for me to say in retirement.

I know full well that it is not easy to demand fair pay. A woman always faces a risk that she will be denied her request and face negative consequences in how she is viewed. Therefore, I would never encourage a woman to do anything unless she weighs the risks and the consequences. I also understand that in some circumstances, it is better to be paid a lesser amount than to have no job at all. As we recover from the Covid-19 pandemic, there may be other factors to consider in addition to pay. For example, being able to work from home or in close proximity to one's home may be more important than actual wages.

Another thing that women don't do often enough is negotiate stock options as part of their compensation. An article in the 2021 Women in the Workplace section of the *WSJ* concludes: "Women often don't know what to ask for, experts say. And companies don't tell them."[21] According to the report cited by the *Journal*, "[T]he average value of company shares held by male employees in 2018 was $104,902. For women, it was $26,361." Brooke Harley, a former corporate attorney, Lululemon executive, and now CEO of ClassRebel, an e-learning company, said that if women gained more stock options as part of their overall compensation, "That would be the life-changing thing at the end of the day." I couldn't agree with her more!

For me, unequal pay was more than about the money; it was about fairness and respect. If a woman does not respect herself by standing up and demanding to be treated justly and equally, then no one else is going to respect her either. Self-respect—not money—is what will matter to many women in the end. In addition, every woman who demands fair pay is helping other woman to be treated fairly in the future. We do not want to wait for another forty years until women are paid equal to men.

THIRTEEN

The New Millennium—Still Second-in-Command

After my husband's death in 1997, I was exhausted and in the depths of grief. I felt beaten down from all the years of fighting and losing—fighting for my husband's life, fighting for equal pay, fighting for recognition, fighting to be heard and acknowledged. I was finding it more and more difficult to maintain the upbeat, positive attitude my mother had instilled in me.

I had a decision to make. I was fifty-two and had many financial obligations, due to my husband's illness and death. I was three years away from early retirement from United Airlines. Would I leave the company and start over somewhere else?

I owned five houses (several in disrepair) and two entrepreneurial businesses. Because of my husband's protracted illness, sales taxes on my antiques business had not been paid and the IRS was becoming impatient. Hospital bills (many of which I contested) resulted in calls from collection agencies.

Without the continuing support of Randy, the CIO, I don't know if I would have survived. He sent staff to my home with orders to help clean up the home and grounds where I lived—a task beyond their futile attempts. His kindness and that of my staff helped me to decide to stay—at least for a while. While this decision may have appeared to be another copout, it turned out to be a good one for me.

Gradually, I became interested and motivated by my job again. In the aftermath of my husband's death, I had lost interest in climbing the corporate ladder ... or maybe I just felt it was hopeless to continue trying. Randy moved on, and I was left with an organization whose mission was to sell United's technology solutions around the world. I began traveling abroad again.

○ ○ ○ ○

As we moved into the new millennium, many more women were reaching higher levels in corporations, and I hoped they would not have to face the same level of discrimination I had encountered in my career. At the very least, I couldn't imagine any woman being asked to enter through a back door to attend a business luncheon. Now the offensive and unfair things I saw happening to women in the workplace were much subtler than the blatant discrimination I had been subjected to earlier in my career. As an example, one of the women in my division, who was now a peer, had a vague resemblance to me. Lana and I were approximately the same height and weight, with medium-length blonde hair. The resemblance ended there, however. Our facial features were not similar, and it was hard for me to understand how our male colleagues could mistake one of us for the other. Yet we were often called by the other person's name, even though we didn't have the same responsibilities. I cringed whenever I was referred to by my colleague's name, because I felt we were being lumped together in a category of attractive, blonde-haired women. Thus, I still didn't feel confident that I was being recognized and valued for my unique contributions.

After my husband's death, I tried to ignore these subtle slights. His death had made me appreciate how valuable life is and how important it is to be happy. As I grew more at peace with myself, I began to value the opportunity my job gave me to travel around the world, marketing and consulting on computer technologies. I enjoyed getting to know many men and women from various cultures—China, Europe, Singapore, Japan, Israel, and South America to mention a few. The professionals in these other countries seemed much friendlier to me than the business people in the U.S. Why was this the case? I often wondered. Did business people in the U.S. treat foreigners in an equally welcoming way—especially if they were women?

On a break from a meeting in New Zealand, for example, I told a young man how worried I was that one of my dogs was having panic attacks ever since my husband died. He whisked me off to a health food store, where he showed me a homeopathic solution called Rescue Remedy that he gave to his son before exams. I tried it on my dog later. Whether it was the solution or the passage of time, she seemed to become calmer.

While visiting Hong Kong, a colleague introduced me to his sister. She taught me everything she knew about pearl necklaces, so I would be educated about them before purchasing one for my mom, Lana, and me.

Sometimes I traveled with a manager from Air Canada who had a wonderful sense of humor. I was often challenged to keep from laughing in meetings because of his dry comments and antics. Another man who sometimes traveled with me, a purchasing manager named Kurt, remains the funniest person I have ever known. While I tended to be serious about my work most of the time, these men made work fun. They also made clients laugh and helped us to achieve great results.

One night after our meetings, a senior manager in Bangkok took me shopping to a bazaar—a bustling, mazelike area I probably wouldn't have ventured to alone without her accompaniment. Another night, after I'd flown into London that day, a client insisted on taking me to a play—most of which I unfortunately slept through. Nevertheless, these heartwarming experiences were such a relief from many of my experiences back in the States.

As I wondered why I valued these encounters so much, I came to several conclusions. First, I enjoyed seeing new places and learning about different cultures. Second, all the people I met were charming and gracious. But probably equally as important, I had changed. I wasn't in competition with these people; we were together to see if we could reach some mutual solutions for our companies. I never forgot that I was selling and that they were buying, but I wanted the best solution for them and both our companies.

By contrast, in all of my other jobs in the U.S., I often felt there was competition between people … especially in meetings. Who would come up with the best idea? Who would embarrass themselves by suggesting something viewed negatively by the other attendees? Constant judgment about speech, attitude, knowledge … and in the case of women, appearance. Constant competition. Little teamwork. The newer tech companies seemed to have addressed these issues, but human nature is still grounded in survival of the fittest.

o o o o

I would say my experience with China was an exception to my international dealings; I don't look back with the same lightheartedness as I do with my other negotiations. I don't remember all the details of why we weren't able to meet in mainland China at Air China's headquarters, but the first meeting was set up at a location of their choosing in Taipei. Usually when I took a trip to sell technology, I had several technical and business experts supporting me. Due to conflicting schedules and other issues, I had only one other person with me on that trip, my favorite purchasing agent, Kurt. He was neither a technology expert nor a lawyer, but Kurt had been with me on many trips previously, and I always found his quick wit, calm demeanor, and sharp insight to be most valuable. And as I said previously, he consistently made me laugh.

When Kurt and I arrived at the meeting in Taipei, we walked into a room to find over twenty businessmen seated at tables in a formation similar to a classroom. They all seemed to be wearing the same dark business suit as they rose in unison to greet us. Kurt and I were directed to be seated at a table facing them in the front of the room.

"I knew we would be outnumbered, but this is ridiculous," I murmured as Kurt and I took our designated seats at the head table.

One by one, the Chinese men introduced themselves and described their functions—legal, technical, contract negotiations, etc. After they finished, I gave an overview of the software we had come to sell. I named our price and how we had come to the figure.

Then several of the Chinese men took turns telling us why they would only pay a small fraction of our price for the software. As they spoke, Kurt seemed to be listening with his usual, calm look of understanding. Meanwhile, I was feeling more agitated by the moment over the unreasonableness of their offer and their unwillingness to negotiate. My annoyance must have shown on my face; I never did learn how to keep a poker face.

"Gentlemen," I said, after they had finally finished speaking, "we couldn't possibly sell our software to you for that small amount of money, particularly when many other companies have paid so much more. That wouldn't be fair to them."

Another hour of discussion went by without any progress being made.

I whispered to Kurt. "I've had it! Let's get out of here."

"We can't just walk away after coming all this way," Kurt whispered back to me.

"I don't care. They're being totally unreasonable." I also became upset that Kurt was not following my lead.

"I'm sorry, gentlemen," I said, as I stood up, "but if that is all you're willing to pay, I am leaving." I picked up my purse, my papers, and my briefcase, and began walking out of the room.

I saw Kurt motion to the men to stay seated. "I will talk to her," he said, in a tone that suggested I was an unreasonable child having a hissy fit. I threw an angry look toward Kurt. I was feeling out of sorts from jet lag and regretting we had come all this way for nothing.

Kurt joined me in another room and tried to talk me into returning to the meeting. I ignored him and continued putting my papers in order and shoving them into my briefcase.

After a short time, one of the Chinese businessmen came into the room, bowed in a conciliatory manner, and said they had reconsidered their offer. In the end, the Chinese offered us a reasonable sum for our software. They had read me correctly … I had been prepared to leave without a deal.

What I clearly saw then (now almost twenty-five years ago) was that the Chinese would become the U.S.'s greatest competitor, particularly in the field of technology. Chinese businessmen were willing to forego short-term gains and make decisions that would not pay off for many years—unlike most American businessmen, who didn't want to wait years for their bonus. While this was an obvious conclusion for me, only recently, in 2021, have I seen many articles reaching the same conclusion. But what are the chances that anyone would have listened to me or any woman raising such an alarm twenty-five years ago?

o o o o

While traveling throughout the world, I was surprised to see so many women working in critical functions, often just below the heads of their companies or organizations. I referred to these positions as "second-in-command;" later in time, some of them would be called "C-suite" positions. Before my travels I had thought the United States was way ahead of other nations in placing women in key positions.

Just as in U.S. companies, many of these women seemed far superior in knowledge and capabilities than the men to whom they reported. I also noticed that many women who were in second-in-command positions did not exude the same level of confidence as their male superiors demonstrated, even though the men in charge often did not have a good grasp of their field and seemed like figureheads. I wondered if conveying a commanding style comes as a result of the position, or if the position is obtained because of how someone presents and carries him- or herself.

Are men born having more confidence in themselves, or is it learned behavior supported by culture? I wondered. In any event, men do a much better job of exuding confidence and authority.

While on a consulting job in England, I got to know a female consultant named Heather, who was as bright and capable as anyone I had ever met. She was also quite outspoken. On many occasions, we ate dinner together.

"I can't get over how in every country I have done business," I said to Heather one night, "women are the ones who lead the projects and do outstanding jobs of performing the day-to-day tasks of keeping their companies running."

"It's truly remarkable, isn't it?" Heather said. "They are probably pleased to have reached the level of responsibility they have achieved, even though their idiotic bosses get all the credit."

"At least you have a woman who is looked upon as royalty in your country."

"That may be true, but believe me, she has minimal decision-making authority. I think your day in the U.S. will come soon. I hope so. It might take a woman to straighten out this mess of a world."

"Seriously, I see men running companies all over the world who don't seem anywhere near as competent as the women underneath them. Am I just imagining this?"

"Hell, no. You don't have to be competent to be a figurehead. You just have to have a big you-know-what and surround yourself with competent people. Unfortunately, we're still at the stage in our development where the majority of us, both men and women, are more comfortable having a man in charge. Just look at what happened when women first became airline pilots. I know some stupid men who actually refused to fly when a woman was the captain, supposedly because they didn't have confidence she would keep a cool head in a crisis."

"Perhaps there is some truth in that. I know I can become pretty emotional at times."

"Sure, we all can. But just think how you've reacted when you've been in a real crisis situation. How have you reacted versus other people you know?"

I thought for a moment. "I guess I can honestly say that I have remained pretty calm. But so have most of the men I know. One of my biggest challenges has been trying to maintain confidence in myself, after being treated with such disregard so often in my career. Sure, there have always been the exceptional men who have supported me. But year after year, the inequity of my pay, my failure to be promoted, and my input frequently being ignored have chipped away at my confidence. Of course I keep working hard, but it is so wearisome to fight these battles all the time and keep my head held high."

"I wonder how women will react when more of us attain top positions. You know the old saying about how power corrupts. I hope the position and associated power don't go to our heads, and I hope we don't treat men like we've been treated—although I'd sure like to see them get a little of their own medicine for a while," Heather said with a mischievous smile.

I nodded and smiled too. "We need to get to the point where gender, just like race, is not a determining factor for business success. We are far away from that now, because most companies are still run by men. And men will continue to choose men over women for top jobs until everyone is as comfortable with one sex as the other."

"I think you're right, Donna."

"There is no question in my mind that women are just as capable of performing all corporate business functions as men. And on average, I think women are more creative than men and are much better at multitasking. I realize that many of the great artists and creative geniuses have been men, but I'm talking about the average person. I also know that many women have never been given a chance."

"It all comes down to how men have managed to maintain control and keep women in their place," said Heather, shaking her head. "I sure hope my two girls don't have as difficult a time as we've had. I think my son was actually born more emotional and sensitive than my two girls. But I can already see that changing. Peer pressure is forcing him to toughen up in the traditional masculine way. Although I've done everything I can think of to not let my girls feel inferior, how can they not look at the world, just as we've been talking about it, and not wonder if there is something inherently wrong with them?"

I leaned back in my chair, folded my arms in front of me, grimaced, and shook my head from side to side. "That's the point I keep coming back to—feeling inferior. Imagine how women of color must feel if I feel so angry."

"I know. Sometimes I feel guilty for complaining when I know that others have had it much worse."

"I do too. But it's horrible to think there is something not as good about you as the other gender in the human race. Even though we are told we are all equals, it doesn't always feel like that. Even the churches in the world promote the idea of women being inferior. I used to belong to the Catholic Church, where nuns can do most everything but celebrate Mass, consecrate the host, and hear confessions—you know, the more important, powerful jobs. Supposedly, the rationale is that the Church needs to continue the tradition established by the first pope, Peter, who was a man. Wouldn't it be just as logical to say that Peter was a human being, and therefore a priest should be a human being?"

"Let's not even get started on that drum," Heather said. "Think of the poor Muslim women. How can those women put up with all that shit, like not being able to drive or go out alone, and having to cover themselves up with a burka? When I think about how all the major religions of the world undermine being female, I get a little crazy."

"So do I. I have met many brilliant Middle Eastern women. I admire women who can gracefully accept their role without the anger and resentment I so often feel."

"That's really what it comes down to, isn't it? Accepting our roles with a grateful heart, while trying to do whatever good we can to help others succeed—especially women."

"Yes, that's it in a nutshell. But it's hard for people like me, who hate injustice and rebel at being treated in an inferior manner. I've had to spend what I think is an inordinate amount of time trying to get over my angry feelings about being discriminated against. I can't tell you the number of self-help books I've read about anger."

"Well, you know how I react. At least you have more restraint. I just haul off and tell the men where they can go."

"Sometimes I wish I reacted more like you, instead of being so polite and politically correct. I could be wrong about this, but I don't get the sense that women from other nations are as upset about playing a secondary role as women in the United States."

"Perhaps they just hide their feelings better."

"Or perhaps our culture in the States makes us feel and act differently. We are indoctrinated with the belief from an early age that we can do anything we want to and be successful. I know that's how I was raised. And then, when we hit those barriers and find ourselves up against the glass ceiling, we are disillusioned. Combine that with being taught we have the right to speak our truth, and it makes for some very vocal, unhappy women in America."

"We have a lot of unhappy, vocal women in England, too."

I sighed deeply. "I think much of my problem stems from the expectations my father set for me. Do you know that in 1976, my dad wrote a letter to me, saying he was sure I was going to be in top management? And then a decade later, he wrote in another letter that he saw me as CEO of a company. I wonder what he's thinking now, as he sees me struggle—from his vantage point in heaven or wherever he is."

Heather nodded in sympathy, then shrugged. "There are a lot of good things about being born female," she offered. "We can wear beautiful clothes. Men buy us flowers and gifts. We are adored and praised. And we can birth babies."

"And who knows what the next generation of women will achieve?" I said, rustling up a smile. "I hope our efforts have paved the way."

Heather and I maintained our friendship after our mutual assignment ended. She was just one of many smart, capable, and refreshingly outspoken women I met throughout my career.

FOURTEEN

Understanding Negative Perceptions

I was never one to actively seek feedback about my performance. I tended to become nervous before formal reviews, worried that I might be criticized. It always surprised me when subordinates actively sought my input. I now look back and think what a mistake it was for me to not aggressively seek input on my performance and how I was viewed, even though many supervisors are reluctant to be forthcoming and frank.

If we are fortunate, at some point in our career, we will have that moment when we get a true glimpse of how we are viewed in the workplace to help us understand what is propelling our career or holding us back. For much of my career, I didn't know for sure where I stood in terms of advancement.

As I moved up the management ranks, I was periodically given tests to ascertain my management style and capabilities. After one such test, I sat in my boss's office.

"You have some unusual test results," he began. "You scored higher than anyone else in the company on quick decision-making. In fact, you are in the ninety-ninth percentile of people who took the same test in other companies."

I sat quietly and didn't know how to interpret his statement. He had come from outside the company about five months previously, so we didn't know each other well.

"Actually, I have been extremely uncomfortable with how quickly you make decisions. You come across as if you've given hardly any time to consider alternatives or the ramifications of your decisions. But as I've watched you, I've realized most of your decisions are sound—in fact, amazingly sound. How do you do that?"

"I really have to think about this," I said, "because I've never been given such feedback, or really thought that much about how I make decisions. I guess I just listen to my intuition."

"How do you define intuition?"

"I just listen to what my gut tells me. Sometimes I hear an internal voice tell me what to do."

My boss nodded thoughtfully. "Well, here's the problem. Whereas I have gotten to know you and have analyzed the results of your decisions, most people just witness how quickly you react; that makes them think you haven't taken the time to think things through. This makes people uncomfortable with your decisions, just like I used to be."

Of course this surprised me, because I had never given my decision-making style any thought. "I can understand that," I told my boss. "I guess most managers weigh the pros and cons for a while before making a decision. I can see how my approach could be viewed as jumping to a conclusion. Sometimes I *do* go back and weigh the various pros and cons of a decision, especially if it's a critical one, but I almost always stick with my original conclusion."

"That's fine, but you need to be aware of how you are viewed. I'm not asking you to change your decisions or the way you come to them, but to think about how you are being perceived. Rather than allow people to think you are too hasty, you might want to wait a bit before presenting your decisions."

"I can't thank you enough for this valuable feedback and insight."

Although I continued to make quick decisions, I did follow my boss's advice and tried to provide more rationale when presenting my conclusions to others.

○ ○ ○ ○

On another occasion early on in my career, I was the only woman in a one-day class. The instructor was trying to assess our management style by giving us a multiple-choice test based on a leadership model developed in the 1960s—the Blake and Mouton Managerial Grid. Before the class ended, she said each of our styles was going to be placed on a grid with 81 possible points; each point on the grid represented our concern for people versus our concern for production. The admired style at the time—and the one identified for most of my male classmates—was high concern for production and low concern for people. Concern for people was viewed as a weak and unproductive management style.

When the teacher announced my test score on the grid, it was radically different from all my classmates. In essence I scored high in concern for production and relatively high in concern for people. Mortified, I felt my face blush as the test results were announced out loud.

I'll never fit in and be successful, I remember thinking to myself. I will never be one of them. I not only wanted to slide under my desk, but I felt some of the men were eyeing me triumphantly, as if to say: "See, we knew you'd never fit in and be a good manager." I don't know whether anyone actually thought something like that, but I was convinced I would always be different and never fit in. I wanted to beg the instructor not to report my numbers to anyone outside of the classroom. I feared if I hadn't attempted to seem less concerned about people when choosing my answers on the test, my point on the grid might have indicated even higher concern for people.

○ ○ ○ ○

Many years later, after thinking I had permanently smashed up against the glass ceiling, I had another opportunity to get some feedback and learn how I was viewed. A woman I knew was being counseled by a consultant, who eventually told her she would never progress to the senior management ranks in her company. The consultant said that one senior officer would not support her and would strongly oppose her advancement. I guess I hadn't totally given up on becoming an officer, because I decided to hire this coaching firm to provide me with some feedback.

The consultants asked me to identify ten people above me, as well as ten peers and ten subordinates, who would be solicited for feedback about my performance, my style, and my effectiveness as a leader.

The results of the feedback, particularly from the senior people, surprised me. The president had said that I was my own worst enemy and that if I ever decided what I wanted to do, I could be very successful.

One of the consultants asked me whether I saw myself as entirely competent and whether I truly wanted to assume a top leadership role. My soul-searching revealed that I was uncertain how to answer those questions.

I realized that I had never seen myself as fully competent, confident, and without question the best person for a top job. I had tendencies toward self-doubt and feelings of inadequacy, despite my many accomplishments (and of course those negative feelings were reinforced by pay inequity, lesser titles, and being ignored in meetings). Sometimes I felt intimidated by the officers and was not as forthright as I could have been. Often I took minor slights personally. Sometimes I cowered before taking up a fight. The consultants also pointed out how my career had bounced all over, from various technical disciplines to marketing and sales, making it difficult for others to see me as an expert in any one discipline.

Rather than just allowing me to blame the men in charge, being told the problem was partially my fault was not easy for me to accept. At the same time, the feedback gave me hope. If the president thought I just needed to decide what I wanted to do, then maybe I could still become a top officer, rather than continuing to stoke my anger at my male superiors for my lack of advancement.

As I continued my soul-searching, I realized that although I enjoyed many facets of business and had been in charge of a variety of disciplines,

I couldn't honestly say I had ever had a job that I could commit to and remain totally interested in for any length of time. My employers had realized this and had always accommodated me by placing me in different positions every two years or so. Whereas most people had clearly dominant talents and leaned toward either analytical or people-oriented fields, I jumped with ease from hardcore technical jobs to the softer skills, such as marketing and human resource management. And not only did I not stay interested in a job for long, I owned two entrepreneurial businesses on the side—an antiques business and a day spa. No wonder I was not viewed as being committed to any one job: I wasn't.

I realized I had inherited my father's trait of frequently changing interests and penchant for starting new businesses. As a young man, he played the trumpet in a band during World War II for four years—a career he thought he would pursue, until the realities of making money and supporting a family set in. Then over a few decades, he owned a gas station, several apartment buildings, a restaurant, a mink farm, a blacktop paving company, and a furniture-stripping business. After selling those businesses at a young age, he became a business manager for two high schools.

From the age of seven, I had been my father's most trusted partner and participated in the planning of all his new ventures. For me, planning a new business with him was as exciting as a ride on a roller coaster. I couldn't wait until the blueprints were rolled out on our kitchen table, and we could start planning.

Fortunately, my shifting interests didn't require me to change companies every year, either because I had found consultant positions at a variety of companies, which kept me engaged, or was placed in new, more exciting roles. But now I was being told that because of my versatility, I was viewed as not being focused and committed.

I also realized that most senior officers I knew had started their careers in a particular field, such as accounting, and had usually stayed in their chosen field throughout their entire career. They thereby earned the reputation of being an expert. My jumping from one discipline to another didn't fit the mold. It was becoming clear to me how I might be perceived as flighty and perhaps not serious enough about my profession. And yet I believed that having a variety of experiences in multiple disciplines, and being adept at handling personnel issues, made me an even stronger candidate to assume the top jobs. Much as I considered my diverse interests, skills, and expertise to be positive attributes, being different from the male norm was clearly viewed with skepticism.

I was not alone in having these varied interests and capabilities. Many women I knew enjoyed working in a variety of disciplines and were good at handling personnel issues. Even women who elected to stay at home to raise children seemed more versatile to me than their working husbands; they managed all facets of their household, from decorating the home and learning the best way to raise their children, to handling the family's finances.

The feedback from my subordinates was more specific to our current organization and useful, in that I was able to act on it and remedy issues. In the end, I decided that I would not have traded having an officer position for all the wonderful jobs I had filled in my career. If sticking to one track to the exclusion of all others was the price to be an officer, I was not willing to pay it.

Unfortunately, I didn't have the opportunity to share the fruits of my self-examination with the consultants. They were eliminated when my company hit financial difficulties. As the company went through successive management changes in a desperate attempt to survive, I was part of an interviewing team that hired the new Chief Operating Officer (COO) who became my boss.

FIFTEEN

Losing a Job

The higher an executive climbs on the corporate ladder, the more important politics becomes—who you know and are friends with. Your enemies and those with whom you are in conflict also become extremely important. I should have realized this when I was introduced to Allen, my new boss. From day one, Allen and I were like a lit match and a stick of dynamite; I was the match. Although I respected his professional knowledge, and even thought him attractive as a man, I found some of his communication with employees and actions to be outrageous.

For the most part, especially during the early part of my career, I respected my bosses for their knowledge and expertise. But as my career progressed and I gained more experience and confidence in handling a variety of situations, I came to regard my skills as more advanced than those of most of my bosses and superiors, particularly the skills of managing and achieving results. I often found myself explaining to them what to do and how to do it. It's not that I thought they were incompetent; rather I just felt I had the experience to better handle certain situations. Although I tried not to let my frustration show, I often felt as if they were inexperienced children in need of coaching and counseling.

In addition to my marketing responsibilities, I led an effort to prioritize all of the technology initiatives for United Airlines; the results were endorsed by top management. Then I became responsible for the relationships and coordination of technology activities between the airline and the Star Alliance—an organization formed to provide smooth transfers among global partner airlines and provide rewards for frequent international travelers. Hence, I was required to do more international travel.

While still reporting directly to Allen, I was given another assignment to establish new goals and strategies for the entire company. In this position I had to work with the CEO, president, and other top executives in the company. At times I wondered if Allen was comfortable with me working with the senior officers, because I was privy to information and discussions he wasn't. Allen must have known that I didn't approve of some of his actions and that I could easily have voiced my opinions to his boss (although I never did that). Given our contentious relationship, I suppose it was inevitable that Allen and I would have an altercation. Although the issue we quarreled over was not a major problem, I considered it a principled one and dug in on my position. He gave me orders, and I refused to obey them. Our quarrel ended in a highly confrontational meeting. Fortunately, an HR representative was in the room.

Two weeks after our tense meeting, I was scheduled for my annual performance review. Even though our offices were in close proximity, Allen and I had not spoken to each other since our confrontation.

"How are you doing?" he asked pleasantly, as I took a seat in his office.

"I'm fine," I said, "but I don't want to have my performance evaluation today. I'm leaving on vacation this evening, and frankly, I don't want to be upset. I'd like to reschedule the review for when I return."

He nodded as if he was not surprised by my request.

"I've always had problems dealing with strong women like you," he said. "Our conflicts are entirely my fault. You push all my buttons. I'd like you to help me," he said, sounding very humble and sincere.

I was dumbstruck. This conversation was the last thing I had expected. I stared down at the notebook in my lap. *So I used to be weak, and now I'm strong*, I thought to myself. *Now being strong is a problem!*

"This is a request," he said, after I continued to sit in silence. "I'd like you to help me. Do you have an answer?"

"I don't know what to say. Of course I'd like to help you, but I think it might be difficult since you are my boss."

"Well, that's the way things are. I think you should look at your evaluation," he said, as he handed it to me. "I think you'll like it."

I quickly read the evaluation and looked up at him. "Thank you," I said. The evaluation couldn't have been better.

○ ○ ○ ○

I came back from vacation determined to be supportive of Allen. Although he may have taken the blame for our contentious relationship, I knew I had been patronizing and antagonistic toward him on numerous occasions—sometimes even in front of his subordinates.

He told me he wanted to do a major overhaul of his division and asked me to help him. After setting the overall framework, he asked me to work out the details. Later, he approved the organizational structure I recommended; he also identified the leaders of the organization whom he planned to eliminate and his reasons for doing so. I was led to believe that I was the only person who knew about the changes.

During this period, Allen encouraged me to interview to be Chief Information Officer of the Star Alliance, which had now become the world's premier consortium of airlines. Since I had already been working with the founding airlines, I had many established relationships. Allen coached me for the interview and led me to believe United's president wanted me to take the job. After having in-person interviews, the then-CEO of the Star Alliance told me by phone that the job would require me to live in Frankfurt, Germany.

Up to that point, I had been interested in the job and felt I was a shoe-in for the position. But I quickly decided I did not want to move to Germany. I found Frankfurt to be a dreary city. And as inconsequential as it may sound, I did not want to leave my two dogs, Mattie and Buffy, or to have to quarantine them for an extended period. The job was enticing, but I wanted to live in the United States. I tried to present all the reasons why I didn't think the job required living in Frankfurt, but I did not feel as if I was making much progress in changing the CEO's mind, though I could understand his desire to create a cohesive team in one location.

○ ○ ○ ○

Of the various tasks I was handling at the time, the most challenging was developing new goals and strategies for United Airlines. Before meeting with the CEO and presenting him with the results of the effort, I needed to meet with all of his subordinates and attempt to gain their buy-in. Some accepted my recommendations and others did not. For example, the executive in charge of on-time performance for the airline thought the goals were unrealistic. I did not gain his acceptance, and I did not agree with the lower numbers that he suggested.

I had just presented my recommended goals to United's CEO, when 9/11 happened ... obviously with severe consequences to the company. The following day I was put in charge of establishing a team of people to interface with representatives of the FBI and the CIA—twenty-four hours a day, seven days a week—using information technology to develop no-fly lists and thwart any future terrorist attempts against our company or its worldwide customers. Data from the agencies were not well integrated at the time, and my technical team was able assist in the integration effort.

Soon after, it became clear that United, which was already in financial trouble, could end up in bankruptcy. All the officers were asked to develop plans for eliminating significant numbers of people in their division. I participated in the planning sessions with all the other directors. The timeframe for any action, if it was necessary, was scheduled to happen some months in the future.

Therefore, when Allen called me into his office and told me that my job and all the positions in my department were being eliminated, I was stunned. The furlough action was not scheduled to begin for weeks, and to my knowledge, no other management position in the company had been cut thus far. My reaction was one of total disbelief.

"I don't think you understand the procedures in this company," I said. "If there are any cuts, they won't happen for weeks. Then employees whose jobs are eliminated will be given an opportunity to perform other roles in the company, if they have the skills to do so. Since I am the sole wage earner in my household, I may want to do that."

"Well, that's not how it's being done this time," he said. "There will be no options. If an individual's job has been classified as nonessential, the person in that job will be furloughed. Those are the rules."

"I know that's not how it will be handled. How many other jobs are you planning to eliminate at my level?"

"Two or three. I'm not sure yet. I want you to stay around and support me like you've always done," he said, in a sincere tone of voice, "but I'm sure you won't have any options."

I stood up and walked out of his office with tears in my eyes, feeling shocked and bewildered. I couldn't believe that this was actually happening to me—a person who had always had glowing performance evaluations. How could anyone even contemplate furloughing someone with all my knowledge and the very person who had been put in charge of interfacing with the FBI and CIA after 9/11?

The idea that I was the first of thousands of employees in the company to be furloughed was a huge blow to my ego. I felt hurt and embarrassed. I suspected that at least one other person who would be eliminated in my division would be my female colleague Lana—the only other high-level female in our division.

I decided to leave the building for a while to calm my turbulent emotions. As I headed out, I ran into an officer from HR.

"How are you?" she asked, in her usual friendly manner, which led me to believe that she didn't know what had happened.

"Not very well," I admitted. "My organization has been eliminated, and I'm being furloughed."

"We can't lose key people like you," she said, appearing as shocked as I felt.

Obviously, she knows nothing about what happened, I thought.

"I promise you I will initiate a conference call this evening with all the officers to discuss this," she said.

The next morning Allen called to tell me my case had been discussed in a conference call with the officers. He said all the officers had agreed to eliminate all non-critical jobs, as well as the people in those jobs, regardless of their performance.

What I suspect, although I have no facts on which to base this, is that he put forth a strong position as to how things should be handled, and none of the other officers wanted to challenge him. Perhaps he even went so far as to put his job on the line. I don't know. That's pure speculation on my part. In hindsight, I believe Allen thought his approach was the best way to manage eliminating people in the company.

Perhaps I should have gone to the senior team and pleaded my case. I had more established relationships with the senior team than Allen had, and I had gone above my bosses before. I don't think it would have made any difference, however, because my job was not critical for the company's survival, and Allen's job was.

As I predicted, Lana was ordered to clear out her desk immediately. In terms of acting like a strong woman, Lana made me look like a pussycat. Most likely, the reason she was treated so callously on this occasion was due to her strong demeanor; whereas I was invited to stay for two more weeks to clean out my belongings. There were no other furloughs in our division at our level.

I later learned that most top performers in the company were not furloughed at the time, including several in my organization. As I had thought, no organization would eliminate their best workers. Moreover, in this day and age, how could an executive possibly eliminate the two highest females in a division, resulting in only men remaining at the top level ... and get away with it? Several women later told me that this became a topic of secret discussion among many females, as Lana and I were well known throughout the company. But at the time, everyone was just trying to keep their jobs.

Before leaving the company, I signed a contract, the contents of which I agreed not to divulge. I did not feel good about signing it. But given all of the anticipated layoffs in the company, I figured that my chances of winning a discrimination lawsuit would be slim. The fact is, my primary role in the company was not a critical operational function, and the sales targets for my organization were not being met.

○ ○ ○ ○

For the first time in my life, I stayed home in bed for days without having an illness of some kind. I was devastated. I had let my job become too important, especially after my husband died. My whole identity and reason for living were tied to my job. I had no social life, and all my friends were working. One day Allen called me at home to see how I was doing. Of course, I said I was fine.

Many months later I received a letter from a law firm that I and twenty-four other high-level executives, including past presidents and CEOs, had hired to represent us in bankruptcy negotiations with United Airlines. At the time, I was surprised to have been asked to join the group seeking legal representation. As I looked at the other names copied in the letter, I realized I was the only female addressed in the letter. All the other addressees were men who had been top executives.

As upset as I had been since being furloughed, I immediately felt grateful that at least I would be able to retire with some benefits. I thought of all the men and women who had been fired, furloughed, or forced to leave the company, who would never have the same opportunity. My gratitude allowed me to see my life much differently and feel thankful for what I still had. It marked the beginning of my healing.

SIXTEEN

Becoming CEO

I was now in my mid-fifties—not a sought-after age in the fast-paced, quickly changing worlds of technology and consulting. I decided to wait a while before starting to look for another job; I felt I needed time to rest and recuperate from the stress of losing my husband and now my job.

I had neglected my antiques business since my husband died, and tending to it helped to keep me busy and provided nourishment for my soul. I would go from room to room, spending hours arranging and rearranging all the beautiful displays in the store. I would fondly clean an exquisite Victorian vase or polish an old piece of furniture. My antiques shop was my escape from the disappointments of the corporate world. It was feminine and elegant and beautiful—so different from the masculine, corporate world of business.

In addition, for the past ten years I had served on the board of directors for the United Airlines Employees' Credit Union (UAECU—later renamed Alliant Credit Union). It was the sixth largest credit union in the U.S. based on asset size at the time, and the ninth largest financial institution in Illinois. When I was first asked to join the board ten years earlier, I suspected that I had been selected to be the token woman because there were no other women on the board. I credited my math degree, MBA, consulting assignments, and positions at United for my having received the offer. But now there were two other women on the board. Over the years I had led several board committees and in

February 2002 was named chairperson of the board.

About six months later, a dramatic turn of events took me totally by surprise. The CEO of UAECU suddenly resigned, and a few days later the board asked me to fill the position until a new CEO could be found. Did I suddenly have a fairy godmother watching over me? I wondered. Thrilled, I saw it as an opportunity of a lifetime.

The board set my salary to be the same as the prior CEO's pay—a far larger salary than I had ever earned and one that I thought was more than fair. On top of that, I didn't have any of those demeaning "acting" terms in front of my title. I was CEO, period, even though it was an interim position. I readily accepted the fact that I wouldn't be considered for the permanent CEO position, because I didn't have an extensive financial background.

Employee morale had been greatly shaken due to the prior CEO's sudden resignation. Another board member was put in charge of finding a permanent CEO replacement so I could focus on running the company. I immediately began conducting employee meetings to reassure the employees and to listen to their feedback; I tried to include every employee in these meetings, whether in person or via conference call.

In very short order the senior team came to me with a proposal to expand the membership of the organization beyond just United Airlines. The board had not been privy previously to their proposal. With United in financial trouble, the expansion made sense to me. The UAECU already had global membership, and including companies beyond the airline industry could only strengthen the organization. I believed the credit union could not afford to wait for a new CEO to be found to address the company's future. Working with the senior vice presidents, I developed a case for expanding membership. Although controversial, I believed the changes needed to be made soon in order to avoid financial damage to the company's stakeholders. At an offsite meeting, I impressed upon the board members the need to act quickly. They accepted my proposal.

Of note is that even though I had only a general financial background through my studies in obtaining an MBA, I felt totally confident in the role of CEO: I knew enough about the financial world to get by; I knew how to elicit the best advice from subordinates; and I felt comfortable making major decisions. Moreover, by taking immediate action, I believed thousands of people might avoid financial losses.

After receiving approval from the board to expand the company's mission, I met with one of the senior vice presidents. "You've done more in the past six months than has been accomplished in many years," he said, openly praising my efforts.

I was flattered. "As a board member," I replied, "an individual doesn't have all the facts and understanding that a person gets when working every day in a company. Thanks to you and your colleagues, I have a much more thorough understanding of the issues and what needs to be done than when I was just a board member."

"I can't get over how you went toe to toe with the board members and got them to buy into our recommendations," he said.

"I think the key was that I had no agenda, other than to do what is best for the company. That might sound trite, but I think I'm in a rare circumstance. First, I know I'm not going to remain as the permanent CEO or stay on the board long term. So I have no vested interest in trying to win over the board members or to make them think well of me. Second, my experience of being on the board and getting to know the board members is an advantage. I know what each member's position is likely to be in discussions; I understand their personalities; and I have some insight as to how to handle their objections. Probably, more than anything, at my age and in this stage of my career, I am not concerned about being unpopular. Once a person has fought some of the battles I have as a woman, survived the loss of a spouse, and been let go from her job, there's not much left to lose. I have little to fear."

"It must be a good feeling to be at this stage in your life. I'd like you to give me as much advice and input on my performance as you can," he said.

I was pleased to provide him, as well as my other subordinates, with some of the lessons I had learned during my career. For me, giving advice to young people was one of the most rewarding things I could do.

o o o o

From my vantage point as CEO, I was able to take a broad view of the organization. The organizational chart was typical of many companies, in that all of the senior positions were held by men. It was common knowledge that the board wanted to see more women higher in the organization and wanted women to be interviewed for the CEO replacement. Unfortunately, the recruiters found it difficult to find women with the leadership experience and financial background we were looking for who did not already hold top positions in other companies.

This led me to wonder, as I often had in the past, whether recruitment isn't a big part of the problem in addressing diversity. If qualified women are not presented in the interview process, they can't be hired. Conversely, I had been asked to interview for jobs during my career that I didn't think I was qualified for; I assumed those companies felt compelled to interview women, and I met some of the qualifications.

o o o o

After I broadened the company's mission, I now had more time to focus on day-to-day issues. Actually, there were not a lot of issues that needed my attention, because overall the staff was highly qualified. Part of my job as CEO was to keep from interfering in situations where I wasn't needed. Thus, I had time to sit in meetings and observe the general culture of the organization.

What I found was typical of many male-dominated organizations: the men were clearly in charge and set the tone. Although most of the men were considerate of their subordinates and conscious of their own styles, some demonstrated the old command-and-control style of intimidation, where mostly no one talked except them; their monologues would continue for an inordinate amount of time, and they were clueless about their style. I scheduled these men for training sessions to learn how to manage in a collaborative manner.

When an organization is run predominantly by men, the characteristics of masculinity permeate the organization. The same would be true if only women were at the top—an aura of femininity would pervade the organization. It seems many men are not aware of the culture they establish, or perhaps they don't care. Often, women in male-dominated organizations are viewed as enablers versus leaders, which I found throughout the world where women were second-in-command.

Some of the female attributes I brought to my job as CEO are strengths that other women share. Many women are adept at using collaborative processes (a style that was scorned not that many years ago), and their nurturing instincts, if used appropriately, can provide the necessary support for employees as actions are implemented. Many women have a sharp intuition about trends and other nuances in business environments, and keen insight into the dynamics of relationships. These female strengths are highly beneficial for team building and for a company as a whole, which explains why women shouldn't be pressured into giving up their feminine side to imitate a masculine model. We need both "masculine" and "feminine" attributes to create balance in the workplace.

○ ○ ○ ○

One of the highlights of my time as CEO occurred at a conference with about two hundred peers from other credit unions. As my company was one of the largest in the industry and usually earned top ratings, these CEOs wanted to understand the reasons for my company's change in direction.

As we sat in the large conference hall, the session was opened for questions and answers. One of the CEOs raised his hand and then stood, turning to face me. "I'd like to ask Ms. Fridrych about her experience as CEO and hear any advice she might have for the rest of us," he said.

I rose from my chair to acknowledge his request and took a few seconds to formulate my response. "As you all know," I began, "I am in a rather unique position, in that I am not a candidate to be the permanent CEO of my company. As a consequence, I have no need to impress anyone or gain anyone's support. I am not focused on increasing my salary or seeking a big bonus. My only agenda is to do the right thing for my employees and customers." I paused to look around the room. "Unfortunately, most CEOs worry about their own standing. They tend to spend time and energy fighting off foes—real or imaginary—who want to take their job. In making decisions, they consider how actions will affect their standing and bonus ... all this, in addition to worrying about competitors, employees, customers, and shareholders. The best advice I can give you is to not let your decisions be influenced by how they may affect your personal standing in your company—not an easy thing to do, I grant you."

More specific questions from other CEOs followed. The reason I cite this as a highlight of my career was because of the respect and attention I received from the mostly male audience. As I gazed out at the group, I could see they were interested in my opinions—a far cry from being ignored and feeling invisible in meetings. Although they may have been surprised by my answers and may even have dismissed them, I felt truly seen, heard, and respected. And yet I knew the attention I received was because of my position as CEO ... not because of who I was personally or even because they were familiar with my accomplishments.

During my tenure as CEO, I felt free to act and be who I was. It was such a relief to not have to worry about fitting into the good-old-boys' club. I felt entirely competent and proud in the knowledge I was doing an excellent job.

○ ○ ○ ○

I held the post as CEO for more than a year until a new CEO was found. Although the recruiters said they had tried to find qualified women, the position ended up being filled by a man. I supported the decision because he was the most qualified candidate presented for the job.

My colleague and friend Lana, who had taken a senior job in another state after we had both been furloughed, wrote in a congratulatory card she sent me: "You did it. You showed them. You got it all."

Perhaps I did, but at what price? I asked myself. I felt a great deal of satisfaction in knowing I had fought my way from being excluded and ignored, to CEO of a financial institution. But the road I traveled was not easy and not one that I would like to see other women have to travel.

After all my years of wanting to be a top officer, it had finally happened, and at a time when I had given up hope and wasn't trying to get ahead anymore. How did my father know thirty years earlier that this was going to happen? I wondered. Was it his faith in me and his positive expectations that helped to make it a reality?

There were definitely some unforeseen circumstances that led to this achievement. The resignation of the prior CEO was unexpected and out of my control. But working diligently for ten years as a board member, and conducting myself in such a way that the other board members respected and trusted me, were key factors that were under my control.

The opportunity to be CEO wiped away much of my anger over previous injustices, and I realized it was important for me to look back on my career and forgive all the men who, in my mind, had treated me callously. As I reflected on my many experiences and focused on forgiveness, I was really doing this for myself. I knew that I would be the one to benefit from forgiving anyone I perceived to have discriminated against me. I also knew that I had been given an extraordinary opportunity to heal by becoming a CEO—an opportunity that many women will never have.

SEVENTEEN

Looking Back

Was it worth it? Would I do it again? These are questions I asked myself as I looked back on my career.

I had (and still have) a driven, Type-A personality. I suspect most women who make it to the top have ambitious personalities for varying reasons—to please parents, to bolster confidence, to feel powerful, to change the world, among other motivations.

My answer is yes—I would do it all again because I *had* to. I wouldn't have felt fulfilled if I hadn't at least tried to reach the highest levels possible. As far back as I can remember, I was always competitive—in sports as a young girl, in school for top grades, and obviously in business. Was I born that way or was I shaped by influences during my early years? Was it genes or memes? Probably both played a role. But given my competitive and ambitious nature, making it to the highest levels was important to me.

Of course, there were sacrifices—most notably, the time I was not able to spend with family and friends. The fact that my husband and I didn't conceive any children was not a career choice; it was a result of my husband's illness, my age when I married (thirty-two), and the newness of infertility treatment. Fortunately, I was able to look upon the many women and men I helped in their careers as my children … my family. This was my path, and I have few regrets. I took the advice of a spiritually minded astrologist who told me that my astrological chart was filled with feminine love and nurturing; I chose to use these qualities to help people at work.

○ ○ ○ ○

Time and a new perspective heal all kinds of wounds. Thankfully, we can learn and grow from our experiences. I now see the hurtful situations and incidents of my past in a new light; in most cases my male bosses and colleagues were just doing what they thought was good for business and acting how they thought an executive was expected to act. During my entire career, all of my bosses were men, except for one woman who was technically the boss of my boss. She promoted me one time when my boss was out of town. I had the feeling she delighted in giving me that promotion.

I have forgiven my boss who furloughed me; he most likely believed he was doing the right thing by letting go an employee who was not performing critical work for the survival of the company. And he was right—my job was not essential at the time. My life may actually have been extended by losing that stressful job; many of my male colleagues, who were not furloughed at the time, died in their sixties before having much time to enjoy their retirement. Had I not been furloughed, I would not have been free to assume the CEO position. The universe works in mysterious ways on our behalf. We never know what good things may come out of what we perceive as bad things happening in our life.

○ ○ ○ ○

Aside from the discrimination I experienced throughout my career, there was much I loved about my jobs. I loved the challenge of writing computer programs; I was overjoyed the first time a program worked and didn't get hung up with any errors. I loved building strong teams of people and leading them to achieve important goals … like E-Ticket™. Later in my career, I loved the thrill of negotiating deals and seeing everyone happy after a contract was signed, especially when each participant felt he or she had reached a good deal for their company. I enjoyed working with top managements and helping guide the direction of companies and employees.

Many of the situations that stand out as the most rewarding of my career were the times I connected with and helped my employees. One highlight that brings me great joy to remember was a conference that I conducted, along with my management team. Our main purpose was to honor the employees for their hard work and accomplishments, while also having some fun. Just seeing their expectant, happy faces from the stage where I was presenting was such a heartwarming experience.

Another situation that stands out in my mind was my ongoing communication with a capable young man who was having problems dealing with decisions he'd been asked to carry out in his job. The solutions were not one hundred percent accurate, and this bothered him. Total accuracy was impractical and unfeasible, while doing nothing would have caused havoc. As I counseled this employee many a night after business hours, his confidence returned and his anguish diminished.

Perhaps because of my own struggles, I particularly enjoyed trying to help women and other minorities. Those employees who came to me with open minds and egos firmly set aside were such a delight to work with; I took great pride in their accomplishments and advancement.

That's not to say that I wasn't excited when I received a promotion or raise myself. When that happened, I couldn't wait to tell my husband and my parents. Seeing my parents, who had sacrificed for my education and who had always supported me, take pride in my successes are memories I will always cherish ... that day that Mom watched me on stage in New York when I received the YWCA Woman-of-the-Year award ... Dad's delight in every raise and promotion I received. I only wish my dad and my husband could have seen me become CEO, but they were probably cheering me on from their vantage points in the afterlife.

I also fondly remember the late-night discussions with colleagues in the many companies where I worked. The camaraderie and mental stimuli were so much a part of why I loved my business career.

Finally, being CEO was *the* highlight of my career. How fortunate I was to end my career on such a high note. With that achievement, many of my hurts and slights of the past faded into distant memories.

As for regrets, I have several—most of them focused on what I should have done differently: I often did not stand up for myself and face head on situations of discrimination. I allowed myself to be abused by low pay, inadequate titles, and working too long with an "acting" title. I look back at discrimination as abuse—abuse of power by those in charge. I regret *allowing* myself to be used and disrespected. I no longer blame others for the abuse; I blame myself for putting up with it … for not taking stronger action of some kind, including leaving the positions and the companies where the abuse occurred. I don't want to be too hard on myself, given all the discrimination I faced, but I know I can only change myself.

I regret that I didn't focus more on my communication skills, especially in meetings dominated by men. I wish I had found counselors or psychiatrists to help me understand my lack of confidence in myself. But most of all, I regret feeling as if I wasn't good enough … smart enough … capable enough, because I didn't fit in with the good-old-boys' club. I allowed discrimination to make me feel inferior in some undefined way, when I knew in my heart of hearts that I was more versatile and multi-talented than most of my male counterparts. More than anger at anyone else, I am angry at myself for allowing myself to feel inferior. Of course these feelings are understandable after years of abuse, but my job now is to forgive myself. I'm still working on doing that.

o o o o

After my time as CEO, I wondered what to do next. I had reached a point in my life where continuing to pursue a corporate career no longer interested me. As much as I initially enjoyed my time as CEO, I was astonished at how quickly I became bored, once I had set a new direction and tactical plans were in motion. My theory that the higher an executive climbs in his or her career, the easier the job may actually become, certainly held true for me. Subordinates are usually eager to do anything to impress the boss and win favor by relieving him or her of most menial tasks. A CEO's biggest challenge is to make the best decisions for all stakeholders, and that includes employees. My most important decision as CEO was to diversify the credit union—a decision I am still proud of to this day. Furthermore, as long as buy-in is obtained as part of the decision-making process, the job of a CEO is to step aside and let subordinates do their work, while providing them with the necessary support.

Although I did some further consulting work after being CEO (which I thoroughly enjoyed) and then dabbled with a small retail business, I found my heart was no longer in the corporate or entrepreneurial worlds. As a result of United Airlines filing bankruptcy, I lost two-thirds of the retirement money I had been promised in contracts and which I had begun receiving. Although that was a huge shock, I reconciled myself to leading a much simpler life. I am proud of myself for adjusting my expectations and releasing bitterness and anger.

I began writing ... something I had never contemplated doing. After finishing my first book, which is about my life with my husband (before and after his passing), I began to write the book you now hold in your hands. I would periodically check in with women I knew and had worked with, only to be told that things were not really getting better. They were still dealing with many of the same issues. The women marching around the world in early 2017 confirmed that reality. It seemed hard to believe that after half a century, Gloria Steinem was still marching for many of the same causes.

And now, in 2022, especially as a result of the pandemic, women still have a long way to go ... not only to achieve parity, but in order to make this a better world.

EIGHTEEN

Discrimination Still Exists

Whether you are a man or a woman, a white Caucasian or a member of a minority, you most likely know that discrimination still exists in the workforce to a large degree. You do not need me to quote a series of articles and facts to know that it's true. You just need to know that women hold 8% of Fortune 500 CEO positions in the U.S., which is similar to the rest of the world. You just need to know that women on average are paid 83 cents per dollar of what men earn, and that the wage gap for women of color is shockingly similar to what I experienced fifty years ago.

Large studies have been done in an attempt to explain why discrimination persists and what to do about it—one of the biggest annual studies being the one conducted over the past several years by LeanIn.Org and McKinsey & Co. These researchers conducted interviews at global companies and surveyed thousands of men and women. The results are usually reported annually in a *Wall Street Journal* (*WSJ*) section called "Women in the Workplace."

What this and other similar studies disclose is that, although women comprise almost half of the workforce, what happens to a woman after she enters the workforce is still problematic. Data show that men win more promotions, more challenging assignments, and more access to top leaders than women do. Men are more likely than women to feel confident they are en route to an executive role and they feel more strongly that their employer awards merit

Women, meanwhile, perceive a steeper trek to the top. Less than half feel that promotions are awarded fairly or that the best opportunities go to the most deserving employees. A significant share of women say that gender has been a factor in missed raises and promotions. Even more believe that their gender will make it harder for them to advance in the future—a sentiment most strongly felt by women at senior levels.

In spite of the #MeToo movement, women still face sexual harassment. Women feel bullied at an alarming rate, with statistics suggesting that up to 35% of the workforce have fallen victim to this trend."[22]

Women still don't know how to act to be successful. Investor, advisor, and author Karen Gifford offers further insight. Gifford points out that every woman who has spent time in the professional world has received advice to "Try to look, act and speak as much like men as possible."[23] But she refutes this advice: "If it worked, by now the professional world would look far more coed than it actually does."

Susan Hertzberg, who stepped down after six years as CEO of Boston Heart Diagnostics Corp., reflects my own experiences in an article published in the *WSJ*: "I'd be in a meeting and make a point, and it was as if I was invisible. But the person next to me, who might be male, would rephrase what I just said two minutes later, and the other meeting attendees would think that he had just invented water."[24]

The 2016 study by LeanIn.Org and McKinsey & Co. found: "Not surprisingly, a large share of women feel invisible at work, compared with male colleagues. From ordinary meetings to executive offices and boardrooms, many more women than men feel that they don't get credit for their ideas, or that their contributions aren't recognized—slights felt even more acutely by women of color."[25]

Much of the 2020 study by LeanIn.Org and McKinsey & Co., and reported on in the *WSJ*,[26] focused on the damaging effects that Covid-19 has had on women in the workforce, especially burnout, because women have taken up much of the burden for caring for households and children at home during the pandemic.

However, the 2021 study by McKinsey & Co. and LeanIn.Org. (I find it interesting that the order of the two companies' names has been reversed this year), found some encouraging trends: First, women made strides in white-collar jobs at every level; and second, companies are wooing women back to the workforce with innovative programs. These findings support my belief that women are the leaders of the future.

While this is great news and a positive sign, discrimination against women in the workplace will most likely continue, with many of the same issues I faced during my career. Though there may be many reasons discrimination will persist, I believe there is one prevailing reason: Men do not want to relinquish their power. Ever since the Industrial Revolution, men have been the dominant leaders of big business. Before that, they were considered to be "head of the household" and afforded legal and other rights well before women obtained them. They have enjoyed the privilege of leadership for centuries. Although this privilege was primarily claimed and shared by white men, more men of color have made strides during the past few decades, posing a threat to white supremacy.

What man wouldn't be disgruntled if he was passed over for a position or promotion, especially if it was given to a woman whom he perceived as less qualified? Even if a man respects the woman promoted, he will most likely have some feelings of resentment. And who wouldn't be resentful if he lost his job in a cutback action, especially if he believed he was more qualified than the employees who retained their jobs?

Imagine for a moment that you have been in power for eons ... that you have been a CEO or part of an executive team for a long time, and that you expect that reign to continue. You've enjoyed the privileges and benefits that men have been afforded for decades. Then suddenly, you see all these women being educated and obtaining advanced degrees. "At the close of the 2020-21 academic year, women made up 59.5% of college students, an all-time high, and men 40.5% ...[27]." Women are also graduating at a higher percentage than men, and if the trend continues, in a few years two women will earn a college degree for every man.

Women also tend to perform better scholastically. "The average collegiate grade-point average isn't tracked regularly, but according to data from 2009, it's about 3.10 for women, versus 2.90 for men."[28]

Then, instead of women holding only 5% of CEO positions at Fortune 500 companies (as it has been for years), the percentage jumps up to 8%. Women like Mary Barra run companies in positions from which women have been traditionally barred. Studies start to show that women do a better job of leading a company than men (particularly in terms of profitability).

While most men are probably unaware of many of these statistics and facts, some recognition of these trends most likely creeps into their awareness. Certainly, a woman running a major automobile company is most newsworthy.

Some men would cry "reverse discrimination" and try to maintain their power. That is human nature. Yet the case for female leadership is becoming stronger by the day.

An article in the *WSJ* in January 2021 referenced a new kind of leader that will be in demand—a leader who is not a business guru, but one who is a coach and nurturer. Finally, the strengths that women possess will be recognized and in demand. Certainly education and experience will be required; but the collaborative skills that so many women possess will be sought after and highly valued.

Men will continue to resist giving up their power and domination. Just as we saw resistance from those who lost the 2020 political election in the U.S., all kinds of tactics will be used. That is to be expected. It can be ego-bruising for men to accept that women are every bit as good at doing jobs men have traditionally claimed, and often perform even better.

Nonetheless, I believe the reason women will win the discrimination battle is because they possess the leadership skills of the future. Women now have logical, analytical skills combined with intuitive, collaborative skills. As more companies realize the power of female leadership, more women will be put in charge. It is inevitable. The bottom line will win out.

It takes time for those discriminated against to relinquish their hurt feelings about being treated unfairly. Women and minorities have come a long way in terms of education and attaining prominent positions. But in spite of this trend, we have a long way to go until discriminatory feelings and actions are totally eliminated, and perhaps even farther until women and minorities feel truly good about themselves and how they are treated. In order to feel good, women must give up the hurts of the past and not react too much to current slights. They must focus on their vision for themselves and the future ahead.

The real issue is whether women want to become the leaders of the future. Is the work and effort worth the rewards? It is a personal question and decision.

NINETEEN

Yourself: The Final Barrier

As I review the psychological and emotional issues that I experienced during my career, I realize that women themselves often present the biggest obstacle to their own success. We are afraid of power; we allow ourselves to be bullied; we shirk being visible, and we think we have to change ourselves to fit into the good-old-boys' network. What a shame. We know we can do the job; we prove we can do the job; but we don't feel comfortable with ourselves. I was shocked when I got the message that I was my own worst enemy during one of my last corporate jobs. As important as any degree or credential, self-analysis is critical for any woman who wants to pursue a leadership role.

One of my biggest weaknesses (and one I didn't acknowledge for many years) was that at some level, I did not want to be recognized … to be visible. Obviously, this attitude is a detriment in obtaining leadership roles. I can trace the desire to remain invisible to my childhood and early adulthood. "Women should be seen and not heard" used to be a popular saying. Invisibility for women is often linked to sexuality and shame; both were issues for me. I have decided to explore this topic in depth in another book.

I had less of a problem being visible with subordinates, most likely because I felt accepted by them, whereas I never felt fully accepted by those in authority. I had many issues with authority figures; I did not want to be dominated by men and told what to do by them—a holdover from my father's domineering ways. Obviously, this became an issue for me during my career since almost all of my bosses were men.

Just being acculturated as a woman is enough to undermine anyone's confidence. Most countries on Planet Earth undervalue feminine skills. Men have not intentionally set out to diminish women; they have been conditioned as well by a culture of male superiority. I don't blame men; I blame the culture that we have all been born into.

I share these issues of lack of confidence and a desire to be invisible because women tend to share many of the same internal demons.

o o o o

In July 2020, Jennifer Palmieri published a book titled *She Proclaims*.[29] She was the Director of Communications of Hillary Clinton's 2016 presidential campaign and held several other prominent roles in government. Of all the books I have read about women in business, this is one of the most profound. In essence, Ms. Palmieri argues that women should stop trying to fit into a system that was established and run by men for their own benefit.

I couldn't agree more. I wish I had understood the futility of trying to fit into a man's world—my continuous desire to be accepted for who I was in the good-old-boys' club. That could never happen, because it would change the rules of a man's game. Like Ms. Palmieri, I believe women should stop trying to fit into that mold. By establishing their own rules, I believe women will do an even better job of leading their companies, countries, and the world to a better future.

Instead of a woman lamenting the fact that she is not part of the good-old-boys' network, it is time for women to start celebrating that fact. We should remember that the time has come for a new kind of leadership—women's leadership. It goes without saying that if a woman wants to have a successful career, she needs to prepare herself with several tools to make that climb easier:

- education and experience;

- a personal life that supports her career goals;
- an effective management style.

Since women currently earn more than half of the professional and graduate degrees in this country, a lack of education is no longer the hindrance to securing the top jobs that it was in the past. Gaining experience in various disciplines is also not quite the barrier that it used to be, because women are being allowed to perform jobs in professions that once were considered primarily for men, such as engineering, manufacturing, and construction. But getting the right education and experience to pursue your dream career can still be difficult.

One of the biggest problems for many of today's bright and ambitious young women is not having the funds, scholarships, or other means to attain a higher-level education. However, more options are becoming available for women. Many companies will provide monetary assistance for education and training, particularly to those demonstrating the willingness to work hard. Many companies are also instituting mentorship programs for women, realizing that women in leadership roles improve their bottom line. Even the U.S. government is considering various options to support women's efforts to gain an education.

More men are beginning to support their wife's career, making it easier for other men to do so. We now have new role models provided by the 8% of women leading Fortune 500 companies.

Women will need to address subjects like menstruation and pregnancy in the workplace. Not much has been said about accommodating women during those few days a month when hormonal changes may be affecting them. Perhaps women have been forced to downplay this issue because of negative attitudes and beliefs about women being emotional and incompetent—a bias or prejudice that they have internalized in their own belief system about what it takes to be a professional.

Menstruation is a touchy topic, as it is personal, and some women are more affected than others. Be that as it may, mood swings and pain can be accompanying factors (both were issues for me). It is time to have this discussion in an honest, forthright manner. There may also be physical, energetic, and emotional changes during pregnancy that affect a woman's performance and that need to be openly discussed.

Some people may wonder: why should a company have to make any accommodation for such matters? One reason is that it is a fact of life, just as it is a fact of life that many women today need to work to support themselves and their families. We need women in the workforce for our economy to be fully productive. Another reason is that by not accommodating women's special needs, a company could be losing out on the best CEO the company could ever have. The choice is to deal with these women's issues or to harbor skepticism and prejudice. There are many potential solutions for handling these facts of life; ignoring them is not one of them.

There are other issues for women aspiring to the top. Arianna Huffington, cofounder and editor-in-chief of *The Huffington Post*, sheds light on the obstacles faced by women in high-level positions: "Women still have an uneasy relationship with power and the traits necessary to be a leader. There is an internalized fear that if we are really powerful, we are going to be considered ruthless or pushy or strident—all those epithets that strike right at our femininity. We are still working at trying to overcome the fear that power and womanliness are mutually exclusive."[30]

I well understand this conflict. I struggled with my own feminine identity, especially when I achieved higher positions. Until I could accept that power and my identity as a woman were not mutually exclusive, I felt uncomfortable with how others might view me, particularly when I had to take a difficult stance; sometimes that meant choosing between the lesser of two evils. Women need to learn that at times it's okay to be tough and hard-nosed, and other times it's okay to be soft and caring. This kind of flexibility is becoming easier to practice now that the stereotypical gender roles are loosening in our society in general.

During my career I was particularly concerned about how my husband viewed me, especially when I took the sometimes difficult stands that are necessary in business. Whenever I had to make a challenging decision that required unpopular action, I could feel myself hardening—almost as if a steel rod had been implanted in my spine. At times, I knew my husband thought I had become too businesslike; I was no longer the shy, demure girl he had married. Even though I know he was proud of me most of the time, I occasionally felt his skepticism about who I had become. Such is another price of rising to the top—the toll it can take on marital relationships.

Twenty-five years after my husband's death, I still feel some guilt over having had such a successful career. Several weeks before my husband's death, I asked one of his close friends if my business success had made him feel inferior, and whether it may have contributed to his illness and death. Although his friend assured me that this was not the case, I still have misgivings, even after all this time has passed. *What if this book is successful?* I ask myself. *What will this mean to my relationship with my significant other?* While men may applaud their partner's success, some will feel less of a man, because men have been conditioned to believe that they should be the breadwinner in the family ... that they should be the powerful one.

In a study about the conflict ambitious women face when it comes to their female identity, co-author and Harvard University economist Amanda Pallais found that "[M]illennial women face an age-old trade-off between their professional goals and their desire to attract a mate. When they believe men are watching, single women are noticeably less assertive and minimize their goals including salary expectations."[31] This study supports the theory about women being fearful of being viewed as powerful.

As spiritual teacher, former presidential candidate, and leader Marianne Williamson wrote in *Return to Love*: "Our greatest fear is not that we are inadequate. Our deepest fear is that we are powerful beyond measure."[32] Although that wisdom was meant to apply to men and women, women are particularly susceptible to this fear because the rise to power is new for us.

Perhaps women have shied away from claiming their power because they view power in a negative light rather than thinking of it in a positive way. We have seen power used in a negative way throughout history, and it's what we often see in the world today. It is autocratic and selfish. It is intimidating and tries to force others to do things against their will and desires. It operates on a model of winners and losers. Its predominant tool is fear.

On the other hand, the use of power in a positive, constructive way is uplifting and kind. It is enabling and nurturing, supporting others to reach their potential. It seeks win-win solutions. Its predominant tool is love.

The use of power in a negative way reflects the frequent abuse of power in the past; the use of power in a positive way reflects the feminine model of the future. The challenge for women is to believe that they are powerful beyond their imagination, and to use that power in a constructive way to benefit all of humanity. This may be the future motivator for women—to lead businesses in order to make a better world.

o o o o

My good friend Lana and I have stayed in close contact for more than thirty years, even though our careers took different paths when we were furloughed by our company early in the new millennium. Lana made the difficult decision to move to a different state in order to take a high-level technology job in the railroad industry. Talk about having to face a good-old-boy network to the first degree!

To relocate was not an easy decision for Lana, because she would be leaving family and friends—her entire support system. Although Lana was married, her husband was not working due to a medical condition.

Being in her late forties, she was not in a position to retire.

Lana had always been a smart, ambitious, and extremely hardworking woman. She knew the value of networking and maintaining relationships with both men and women; she was comfortable making decisions in the best interests of those who depended on her. As a result of her successful career at the railroad, Lana was able to provide a wonderful life for herself, her husband, and her aging parents. She also has always been a champion for women.

While I was writing the final chapters of this book, Lana visited me at my summer lake home, and we had an opportunity to spend some quality one-on-one time together. We spent a good amount of time discussing the issues raised in this book. I'd like to replay some of that conversation for the aspiring young career women I hope are reading it.

"What I see as the problem with many young women today," Lana said, "is that they don't want to be powerful. They would rather defer to the men in their lives."

"But at least they have a choice in what they can do," I said. "Before I began my career, my only choices were to be a secretary or a teacher."

"I know. But I find it frustrating that after everything we've been through, paving the way for them, they choose to sit on the sidelines. They don't want to make difficult decisions, or maybe they don't want to pay the price for those decisions."

"In many ways, it is easier to let someone else do the heavy lifting. Not many people, let alone most women, would have the courage to do what you did in your career. I'm so encouraged to see women in charge of major corporations like IBM and GM."

"I wish you could meet Ginni Rometty. You would really like her."

"You actually know her?" I asked, impressed.

"I got to know her when I was working at the railroad, before she became CEO of IBM. I sent her a congratulatory email when she became CEO, and she personally responded to me. I was a nobody."

I was shocked to hear Lana say that about herself. I didn't say so out loud, but I was thinking that Lana was never a nobody. In my mind, she was always powerful and capable. I believe she has the strongest self-image of any woman I have ever known. When I once asked her how she had gained such confidence in herself (something I often lacked), she said her father had always made her feel competent and capable.

This idea of feeling inadequate, of being a nobody, is the reason why many people are not successful in their careers. Partially to blame is the top-down, corporate structure that reveres those in power and makes those below them feel of lesser value; certainly, the compensation structure in most companies enforces that belief. In reality, everyone is a somebody who has been born to do something only they can do.

Even as I wrote this book, I struggled with feelings of being a nobody. I sent over one hundred query letters—letters to literary agents asking for their support of my book—and received a small number of canned rejection letters, but mostly no answer at all. The same thing happened with a previous book. While I know as an author this is not a unique experience, rejection is not a good feeling, and it certainly doesn't boost my confidence.

As Lana and I sat quietly, eating the salads I had prepared for us and looking out over the lake, I thought about another longtime friend who had been a family counselor. She recently told me that I needed to own my accomplishments, especially when telling my story in this book. She said I diminished myself and made light of my successes. If women like Lana and me didn't own our power, what does that say about other women? I asked myself.

"I wish I could have met Ginni too," I said, coming out of my reverie. "I get the same feeling about Mary Barra and Melissa Mayer, although I've never met them. They seem so down-to-earth. Imagine the power these women wield. I'm sure they've had to make some really tough decisions and choices along the way, but they seem so personable and likable."

"I just wish more women would aspire to positions of authority. Maybe this discussion will encourage me to do more work to support younger women."

I hoped Lana would reach out to younger women, because I knew her support and encouragement would make a difference. Whatever Lana pursued, she achieved.

○ ○ ○ ○

In an issue of *The Oprah Magazine*, Glennon Doyle Melton addressed the issue of women not knowing their desires and not being comfortable stating their desires and opinions.

Doyle says: "But women are taught that the way to be successful and attractive to the world is to be selfless. From an early age, we are conditioned to ignore the voice within when considering who we are and what our goals are, and instead to look outward—to our family, friends, church, community, and even our critics."[33] Doyle goes on to say that our bodies eventually become sick when we don't listen to ourselves; our internal voice stops speaking, and we realize we have lost our way.

Why do I and most women have this tendency to diminish ourselves? I know I have done this my entire life. I tell myself it is because I don't like to brag; I don't want to appear arrogant. It doesn't feel comfortable to talk about myself and my accomplishments. Partially, the answer is conditioning—women have been taught by our male-dominated society to diminish ourselves.

I have struggled to own my accomplishments and feel good about them throughout the entire writing of this book, and to understand why it's a struggle. Of note is that I have much less of a problem owning my weaknesses. I finally got my answer where I get many of my answers—in the shower. If I appear weak and don't brag, there is less likelihood that I will be shot down … refuted. I fear repercussions, pushbacks, and being discredited if I step into my power and claim my accomplishments.

Of course, I expect pushback from many men, but I was surprised to discover that I fear condemnation from women, especially from women I have known throughout my career. I fear they don't see me as a strong leader; as someone who fought the system and won; and most importantly, as a woman who has earned the right to offer advice to other women. I realized that the opinions of women matter much more to me than the opinions of men, underscoring the idea that I respect businesswomen's opinions more than businessmen's opinions.

Another reason I don't like to brag is because I don't like to hear other women brag. So how can I expect other women to like to hear me brag? I have found I am comfortable with simply stating what I believe to be true about myself, without hyperbole or forced enthusiasm in my voice: I was a good computer programmer, designer, etc.

Several years ago I attended a class taught by an amazing woman named Regena Thomashauer, or "Mama Gena," as everyone called her. She has made it her life's mission to understand women and help them to own their power and realize their potential. At the beginning of the class, she asked all two hundred of us women to state our desires; most of us had difficulty doing so. Another exercise required us to brag about our accomplishments, another source of discomfort.

More recently in 2021, I took a class in which two renowned, influential, transformational women—Claire Zammit (Evolving Wisdom) and Jean Houston (Human Potential Movement)—teamed up to teach a leadership course based on feminine principles. During the second module of the class, I experienced a mindset shift and began exploring my truest feelings in writing this book.

There is much more help for women today than was available during my career—real understanding of women's issues and profound help. More and more women like Mama Gena, Jean Houston, Glennon Doyle Melton, Jennifer Palmieri, and Claire Zammit are identifying and undoing the results of women being dominated and subjected to the wishes of men for thousands of years. They are teaching us how to take back our power and become comfortable in leadership roles. They encourage us to help and support each other, as only women can do. Thank God for these women!

TWENTY

Women Are Destined to Excel

You might wonder, in light of all the information I've shared with you: How promising is the future for women in business? To my mind, we have gone beyond the "tipping point." In spite of all the issues and barriers I have written about that women still face today, I believe that women will be phenomenally successful in the future ... and not only successful, but they will hold the majority of senior-level positions in corporate America and in many parts of the world. The reason this will happen is that the attributes most women possess, such as intuition, collaboration, and ability to multitask, are increasingly needed in the world-competitive environment. The analytical and decision-making skills that used to dominate now need to be brought into balance with women's gifts for flexibility, cooperation, and nurturing.

I believe we are on the cusp of a big surge in female leadership—a tsunami that cannot be thwarted. As I mentioned in the introduction of this book, multiple studies have concluded that companies with more women at the top rank high in effective management. Following are just a few of the findings of those studies:

- "Companies with higher proportions of women in upper management achieve higher profits, according to a recent study of 21,980 firms in nine countries by the Peterson Institute for International Economics. Profitable firms where women represent 30% of leaders saw a 15% increase in one measure of gross profit, researchers estimated."[34]

- Another study found: "Women who took over from male chief executives increased sales per employee by about 14% in companies where women comprised at least one-fifth of the workforce."[35]
- A study of 820 large, publicly traded companies found that lower-performing companies had fewer female executives. And "On average women make up 20.2% of top executives among companies that scored in the highest quartile in terms of their total effectiveness."[36]
- "A 2019 study from S & P Global Market Intelligence found that public companies with women in the CEO spot or serving as chief information officer were more profitable and had a stronger stock performance, compared to companies with men in the top job."[37]

∘ ∘ ∘ ∘

The financial bottom line is the reason companies are now starting to woo women. A new style of leadership is wanted. Some countries outside of the U.S., such as Taiwan, have figured out that women of today are better leaders, so already have a much higher percentage of female executives.

Putting women in charge of companies—like Mary Barra at GM and Ginni Rometty at IBM—was done to promote profitability and change, not to be nice to women.

As I have said repeatedly, the "feminine" attributes of collaboration and intuition can make women great leaders. Of course, men can develop and utilize their feminine qualities, as many of them have successfully done in the past. In fact, when you think of many of the great male leaders, their insight, creativity, and intuition are the very things that propelled them to the top and made them so successful—the same skills that many women naturally possess. Developing their feminine skills will be as necessary for men as developing masculine skills has been for women.

Many jobs have already been taken over by computers, especially in manufacturing and factories. As computers, robots, and artificial intelligence become more sophisticated and powerful, they will be capable of performing even more of the masculine, repetitive, linear-thinking types of tasks. Artificial intelligence will do away with many more white-collar jobs. The intuitive and social skills will be more difficult for computers to replicate. Understanding relationships, diplomacy, negotiation, and respect for individuality will be hallmarks of leaders as we increasingly shift toward a service industry and global economy.

Another reason women will be so successful in the future is their ability to multitask and to empathize with different perspectives. Finally, all those years of being a superwoman—taking care of the home, family, and holding down a job—will pay off for women.

At some level, I think men know that women have these innate abilities to multitask and handle multiple forms of input—to focus on detailed tasks and then quickly change gears, viewing a variety of impressions and feelings simultaneously. The days of men dismissing these nonlinear abilities as merely a sign of being scattered and irrational are over. In fact, these same men owe much of their success to these abilities in their female secretaries, who handle so much of their bosses' jobs.

As African American and Latina women continue to increase their education and experience, they will gain more senior-level positions in both business and politics. Hopefully they will quickly gain pay equity as well.

We will see continued pushback against women's rise in the ranks of leadership—especially from men. Only look at the Supreme Court ruling of 2007, stating that a female employee who learns she has been paid less than her male counterparts cannot sue her employer unless she can point to recent discrimination, which the law now sets at only 180 days. The women's marches in early 2017 clearly demonstrated a fear among women that they will lose ground in their decades-long, hard-won advances in the fight for equality. Covid-19 has forced some women out of the workforce, and the 2022 Supreme Court's ruling ending the right to abortion and allowing states to ban the procedure is another potential setback for women's progress.

Be that as it may, I firmly believe women are the leaders of the future. At the end of the day, companies are in business to make money, and women of today have better skills than men to lead their companies to higher profitability. The bottom line will propel women to be the leaders of the future. The only question is whether women want to step up and assume the power that is in their hands.

o o o o

I have several words of caution for women aspiring to be leaders. First, do *not* lead in the same manner as men have done if you want to create a better world. Following the lead of men and mimicking their behavior in business may lead to short-term success, but it will not lead us to a better world or long-term success. Second, do not lead in a strictly "feminine" way. Such leadership will not only miss the mark in terms of success, but too much touchy-feely talk will turn off many men and women as well. A new kind of leadership of the head and heart is needed.

Women need to remember that the game has changed. The world is watching. Younger generations are fighting for a new world and will hopefully support and make decisions for the betterment of not only their companies, but for the world at large.

Men must be included and respected in the workforce as women take over more leadership roles. Many will feel threatened by the rise of female power and need to be assured of their role in the workplace.

o o o o

The baton is being passed from one generation of women to the next … from those of us who fought our way into the business world fifty years ago to the amazing women who now lead major corporations. Imagine what the next generation of women can do! I am certain they can change the world, both in business and politics.

Of course, because I have seen so much discrimination in my lifetime against women, I can't help but feel excited to think that women will finally take their rightful place among the leaders in business and be treated with all the respect and consideration due them, because human nature tends to treat those in power well.

Once women achieve this success, however, their real test will begin. Will they repeat the mistakes of the past? Will they follow the male model of the past? Will they wield their power in favor of women to the detriment of men? Will they allow power to corrupt them, as has been the case with so many leaders in the past?

It may be difficult for many women to accept that it is "game over" ... that they have won their rightful place in the world ... that they have a huge opportunity (and responsibility) ahead of them ... that they will change the way business is done in the future. This is a very recent phenomenon, and it may be difficult at times to see it happening. But it is a real and substantial trend that is just beginning to pick up momentum; it is not a momentary blip. You will begin to see more articles with headlines like these articles in the *WSJ*:

- "Women Gain as Skills Shift for High-Paying Jobs"[38]
- "Rankings Defy Usual Gender Gap"[39]

The latter article states: "Female CEOs at the biggest U.S. firms outearn their male counterparts."

In addition to companies wooing women back to work as a result of the pandemic, there have been some interesting, powerful appointments during this time—appointments that have not made front-page news, but are nevertheless groundbreaking.

In February 2021, the U.S. Chamber of Commerce named Suzanne Clark to be its new chief executive. "Ms. Clark will be the first woman to lead the 100-year-old organization, which has long been regarded as corporate America's principal voice in Washington."[40] In other words, the Chamber could be called the most important business association in America. Ms. Clark is known for her ability to build bridges. She represents the new kind of female power.

Also in February 2021, the World Trade Organization named its first female leader, Ngozi Okonjo-Iweala.[41] Ms. Okonjo-Iweala faces a difficult challenge in reviving the organization's influence, similar to what "glass cliff" women face when they are put in charge to rescue floundering corporations.

In March 2021, Meg Whitman was named one of GM's new directors. With this appointment, GM crossed a threshold: women now make up the majority of the board. Then, in May 2021, the Washington Post named Sally Buzbee as its first female executive editor.

Headlines and promotions for women in top executive positions like these will continue because women are key for an organization's success. I am sure that for a while, many women will have that "deer in the headlights" reaction, shocked by this turn of events and finding it difficult to believe that the long-fought battle is over. Accept these findings graciously, ladies ... it's your ballgame now! You can choose to change the world—or not. You can envision yourself as a leader and then make it happen. And don't overreact if you see a little sign of pushback. Of course that will happen. Most important, forgive the men who may have hurt you in the past in the workplace. Let go of your anger—it no longer serves you and will hinder your evolution.

This rapidly changing world has great potential for the fulfillment of everyone. As women stand up and reach their full potential in leadership roles, my fervent hope is that they will use their positions of power and influence in ways that have not always been followed in the past—with fairness, honesty, and for the benefit of all involved, not just for personal gain. I hope that women leaders recognize any bias they may have and move beyond it to give everyone from all backgrounds, including men, the same opportunities to succeed.

Women of today, I encourage you to let go of the injustices of the past. Are you willing to forgive the discriminatory practices and take the necessary steps to move forward and reach your maximum potential? Are you ready to face your fears and assume power? Are you ready to create a role model that will benefit your corporation, your fellow employees, and the world in which we live? Let's envision a future where every little girl will have a chance to reach her highest potential.

Steps for Pursuing a Successful Business Career

I offer the following steps for you to consider when pursuing a management career. Many of the steps are also applicable if you decide a non-managerial role suits you better.

1. Determine what kind of business or craft interests you and best fits your skills. Utilize resources such as psychological tests, books (*What Color is Your Parachute?*), input from family and friends ... but most important, to decide on the right career, choose something that turns you on!

2. Research the best ways to acquire skills for your chosen field: education, on-the-job training, apprenticeships, self-learning, or a combination of learning opportunities. Read interviews with leaders in your field to glean information about their background, preparation, and experiences they found most useful.

3. Pursue learning your field or craft, and don't let anyone or any circumstances deter you from your education. Note: being sidetracked by personal circumstances may be unavoidable and is understandable, but get back on track as soon as you can.

4. Decide what your dream career looks like: CEO of a large company; boss of your own entrepreneurial business; or a competent, well-paid worker without the stress of a management career ... although all jobs can be stressful.

5. Develop a plan for achieving your dream job, but be willing to make

adjustments along the way. Remember that some adjustments are positive responses to new talents or interests you may discover.

6. If you are considering marriage and having a family, choose a spouse wisely—one who will support you in achieving your goals. Be sure to discuss your goals and needs before you marry, and learn the goals and needs of your future spouse as well, to identify any mismatched expectations or areas of potential conflict.

7. Do research on companies in your field. What percent of employees are women? How many women are in top positions? What kind of support and mentoring programs does the company have in place for women? What kind of reputation does the company have? Do the company's stated values align with your values?

8. As you prepare your resume, seek professional help if possible.

9. When you begin the interviewing process, remember that you are interviewing the company as much as the company is interviewing you.

10. Research average wage and benefit packages in your field. Then decide what compensation and benefits you want, and what you will or won't accept.

11. Consider not revealing your prior salary, if you had a previous job. Simply ask for the going wage.

12. Don't rely solely on a company's written strategies, goals, and policies. During the interviewing process, ask to speak to both lower level and prominent women in the organization; evaluate whether they appear to support your core values and management style. Ask women in the company about their experiences with cross-training, paid leave, and family-support programs. Ask yourself whether you feel comfortable with the interviewers. Do they seem genuine?

13. As you begin your career, learn the basic core competencies of your field, including the male-oriented skills of planning, organizing, decision-making, etc.

14. Tell supervisors about your desire to move into higher levels of management. Ask for advice about the best ways to achieve your goals.

15. Ask for constructive feedback from your supervisors. Don't wait for formal reviews.

16. Take classes and work on areas noted in your reviews as deficient. Let supervisors know you are taking these actions.

17. Determine the management style and demeanor you want to project and practice using it.

18. After learning the basic skills in your field, incorporate the female attributes of creativity, nurturing, and intuition.

19. If your goal is to become CEO, ask for assignments in various departments of the company in order to learn as many key functions as possible.

20. If you think you are being sidetracked or have not found a mentor, ask for feedback … perhaps from the HR department.

21. Search for opportunities to be included on boards of directors.

22. If you have tried your best and don't see yourself making progress in your career, perhaps look into working at another company.

23. Most important: Check in frequently with yourself about how you are feeling—powerful, competent, growing, secure, and appreciated; or weak, insecure, stagnating, and unappreciated. Enjoy the good times, and take steps to address any negative feelings.

24. Don't give in to feelings of discouragement or despair. It's natural to feel anxious or discouraged at various points while building a career; but don't wallow! Do whatever helps you to restore and maintain your positive outlook and energy.

25. Always be true to yourself. Enjoy your work, and be happy at what you do.

Some Lessons Learned

CHAPTER 1
Earning Entry into the Business World

- Get to know yourself—your natural abilities, likes, and dislikes; chances are what you like to do, you are also good at.

- Pursue education and work experiences that you enjoy, while keeping in mind the expectations and skills required in your chosen field.

- Never give up your dreams, no matter how unreachable they may seem. Just keep working hard and obtaining education and on-the-job training that will further qualify you to reach your goals.

- Women can excel at the typical masculine disciplines of logic and analysis, while also enjoying more feminine, creative interests.

- Sometimes, not being good at a craft or skill may be a good thing, because inadequacies may lead us to better things. Even personal challenges and setbacks can have future benefits. Don't be discouraged.

- Always stay alert to signs from the Universe, for It may have bigger and better plans for us than we have for ourselves.

- Parents can help their daughters achieve success by encouraging them to pursue education in math, sciences, technology, and business, particularly if a young girl shows interest or talent in those areas.

o o o o

CHAPTER 2
Blatant Discrimination

- Know that there are kind, exceptional people who will help you achieve your goals. Find them, thank them ... and be loyal to them.
- Be true to yourself. Don't try to fit into a business mold that isn't comfortable.
- If you start experiencing chronic, negative emotions, such as anger, seek professional counseling or explore self-help books on the topic.
- Learn how to stand up for yourself in acceptable, assertive ways.
- If you think you are being unfairly paid, ask for a raise.

○ ○ ○ ○

CHAPTER 3
Sexual Harassment

- No woman needs to tolerate sexual harassment; it is against the law.
- Every woman should think about what is acceptable or unacceptable to her in terms of sexual conduct in the workplace.
- If a woman experiences sexual harassment, she should evaluate alternatives for addressing the issue, such as talking to her supervisor about the incident or contacting the Equal Employment Opportunity Commission (EEOC).

○ ○ ○ ○

CHAPTER 4
Intimidation

- Do not let intimidation by a boss or fear of losing your job influence you to do something you know is inappropriate or unethical, but be sure you are accurate in your assessment and take the appropriate steps as outlined by your company's code of conduct.
- If you believe that you are absolutely right about a controversial issue, test your theory on trusted friends and colleagues.

- Whistleblowers are usually not popular, so you may want to have another job lined up before you blow yours.
- If you decide the whistleblower approach is appropriate, start low and work your way up the ladder. Do not do as I did! I was very, very lucky as to how things turned out for me when I wrote directly to the head of my firm.

○ ○ ○ ○

CHAPTER 5
Responsibility Without the Title, Pay, or Promotion

- Find the men and senior women in the business world who recognize and promote female talent. Listen to their advice.
- If you think you are not being recognized in terms of position and pay for your work, talk to your HR representative. Especially in today's environment, they are bound by law to see you are treated fairly.
- As a last resort, if you feel you are not being promoted or treated fairly, seek legal counsel or contact the EEOC.
- Never lose faith in your abilities. If you are not being recognized, solicit feedback and keep trying—perhaps use a new method or find a position in a new company.

○ ○ ○ ○

CHAPTER 6
Support and Lack of Support (or Worse)

- Many men seem to want to support women in the workforce. Whatever their motives, e.g., helping someone they view as weaker, helping someone they see as talented, etc., their support can be invaluable.
- Women need to set and follow realistic expectations as to how they support each other and avoid being too sensitive to another woman's failure to do so.

- Backstabbing other women will usually not bring that individual success.

- Unfortunately, women who are seen crying at work reinforce the stereotypical image of women being too emotional to handle the tough jobs. Women should not suppress their emotions but rather use discretion as to where and when they are displayed.

- Observe your own thoughts and reactions to female colleagues and supervisors. Most people have prejudices they are not aware of. Awareness is the first step in eradicating discrimination.

- After awareness, learning not to act on past biases and prejudices, and being open to people changing, will lead to more opportunities for women.

- Try to work for companies that provide education and on-the-job experience, and take advantage of the opportunities they have to offer.

- Choosing a supportive spouse and a company that shows its commitment to women through innovative programs for support and promotions will make success at any job easier to achieve.

- If you are striving to become a CEO, do not let yourself be pigeonholed into one business discipline.

- Be persistent in gaining diverse experiences. Don't take "no" for an answer.

- Give women some slack when they are struggling with family issues. Everyone will probably face such issues at some point in their career.

- If you are having trouble balancing a family and a career, seek advice from a coach or counselor, someone objective who witnesses this problem on a regular basis and helps women to find solutions.

○ ○ ○ ○

CHAPTER 7
A Choice: Act Tough or Be Viewed as Weak

- People are capable of cruel and heartless behavior in the business world. Do not condone such behavior, whether the target is a man or a woman.

- Women who adopt a tough demeanor may really be expressing their need for protection and actually appear weak and defensive by doing so.

- Women should feel comfortable acting strong and decisive when circumstances warrant, while appearing nurturing and caring at other times.

- When you see a coworker being openly humiliated and treated unfairly, come to their defense, even if you hold a lower position and your action could potentially harm your own professional standing.

○ ○ ○ ○

CHAPTER 8
Using Sexual Appeal in the Workplace

- If you choose to use sexuality as part of your repertoire, know that your actions will attract mixed reactions from men and other women.

- If a woman uses her sexuality, including provocative dress and actions, to obtain promotions, she will always wonder if she achieved success because of her business acumen. Furthermore, she may not have the confidence to perform her best when she is promoted, or worse yet, she may have bypassed learning some of the more important skills for the job.

- Extreme masculine or feminine attire for women in business is distracting and focuses attention on sex versus the job at hand.

- If a woman wants men to treat her equally at work, she should avoid using sexual wiles to arouse or manipulate them.

- Spending hours each day enhancing your appearance may not be the best use of your time.

- Before entering into a sexual relationship with someone in the workplace, a woman should consider the potential consequences to her job.

○ ○ ○ ○

CHAPTER 9
The Unique Challenge of Meetings

- Develop your own style of presenting ideas and comments in meetings that is confident, but not arrogant, and that can be clearly understood. Practice often.
- Learn how to deal with put-downs and being ignored. Unfortunately, women are often excluded in one way or another. Wallowing in feelings of inferiority, resentment, and anger does not help.
- Try not to take being excluded from a particular group personally. Often the exclusion is not intended. It may be that men are simply more comfortable with other men, just as women are sometimes more comfortable with each other.
- Always be true to yourself, and speak your truth.

○ ○ ○ ○

Chapter 10
Recognition

- Decide when it is appropriate to take calculated risks, perhaps breaking some rules; but never do anything unethical or illegal.
- Know that women have succeeded in the past to reach high-level positions and will continue to do so in the future at an accelerated rate.
- Take the time to celebrate your successes. You've worked hard for them and should enjoy the fruits of your labor.

○ ○ ○ ○

CHAPTER 11
Smacking Up Against the Glass Ceiling

- Men have set the standard for how a person should act at the senior levels of management. A traditional masculine demeanor—e.g., tough, aggressive, brusque—may not be best for the company, its stockholders, or its employees.

- Solicit feedback on how you and your performance are perceived. Know that perceptions are just as important as actual performance and may have nothing to do with your real strengths and weaknesses.

- Analyze and determine whether it's possible to change unfavorable perceptions, or whether a fresh start at another company might be better for your career.

- Women will never fit into the good-old-boys' club that has existed for decades. Do not let your self-worth depend upon that fact.

- If you are overlooked for a position for which you are qualified, don't hesitate to make a case as to why you are qualified and should have the job.

∘ ∘ ∘ ∘

CHAPTER 12
Compensation Disparity

- Before being hired, a woman should determine what's most important to her in a job and negotiate accordingly. It could be salary, just loving what she does, flexibility in work schedules, or many other things. Or she might ask for it all.

- If salary compensation is important to a woman, it is wise to negotiate before accepting a position, because it is much more difficult to do so after the fact.

- Learn to address the many negative consequences that unfair compensation can evoke, such as feeling less valued in the corporation for your contributions.

- If you believe you are being unfairly paid, do not hesitate to present your case to your boss or the HR department, depending upon your particular circumstances. Do not let anger simmer. Be as factual as possible in your presentation.

○ ○ ○ ○

CHAPTER 13
The New Millennium—Still Second-in-Command

- Just being competent in your field does not necessarily lead to top management positions anywhere in the world. Learning to demonstrate an image of authority and successfully playing the corporate game are equally as important.

- Women have come a long way in the last several decades, but are still second-in-command. Some women are breaking through the glass ceiling, however, and as long as they persist, more women will do so in the future.

- Women need to acknowledge the natural effects of discrimination—such as feelings of anger and inferiority—and promote positive feelings of accomplishment and satisfaction in themselves and other women.

- It's important to put grievances aside and enjoy your work.

- Businesspeople should extend as much openness and helpfulness when dealing with people from their own country as they extend to people from other countries.

○ ○ ○ ○

CHAPTER 14
Understanding Negative Perceptions

- One of the best things a boss or peer can do for you is to provide honest, constructive feedback about your performance. Never react defensively to this gift. Accept the feedback with gratitude.

- If you are not being promoted to the levels you think you should be, make a sincere attempt to solicit input as to the reasons for not advancing.

- Develop and follow an action plan to address real or perceived deficiencies in your performance.

○ ○ ○ ○

CHAPTER 15
Losing a Job

- No one is indispensable. Always be ready to move on to another job.

- If you challenge your boss or senior management, particularly over important or controversial issues, you may be putting your job on the line. No one is immune to that possibility—no matter how glowing their performance evaluations.

- Don't let your job become the only or most important thing in your life. It is essential to maintain balance and have other interests.

- Learn the art of resilience. Knowing you can and will bounce back after a setback is a most valuable tool for many of life's challenges.

- Learn how to forgive. There may be many situations in life when the act of forgiveness can avert much pain and suffering for yourself.

- Gratitude is the cure for all ills.

○ ○ ○ ○

CHAPTER 16
Becoming CEO

- Never let past negative experiences determine your future. Learn from them, but expect the best is yet to come.

- A person never knows when an unexpected opportunity may arise. Therefore, it is wise to always be ready in terms of education and experience, while staying attuned to and seeking out potential opportunities.

- Never give up hope. If you are doing a good job, unexpected opportunities and recognition may come your way. Be prepared to joyously accept them.

- Although one would like to think that education, experience, and possessing the necessary skills are the main determining factors in promotions, sometimes being in the right place at the right time, luck, or other positive forces also play a role.

- When interviewing for a job at a new company, carefully review the organizational structure for diversity and interview some of the company's employees to understand the culture. Although possible, it is difficult for most women to succeed in a male-dominated organization.

○ ○ ○ ○

CHAPTER 17
Looking Back

- Don't wait to savor your successes until they are over. Cherish each and every victory.

- Check in with yourself periodically about how satisfied or dissatisfied you are with your career. If you are unhappy, evaluate what changes you can or are willing to make.

- You can find satisfaction even in your failures. Your failures may lead you to your next success.

CHAPTER 18
Discrimination Still Exists

- Women should expect that they will encounter discrimination because many men will want to maintain their positions of power, as they have done for thousands of years.

- Every woman needs to decide whether the path to become a business leader is worth the effort.

CHAPTER 19
Yourself: The Final Barrier

- Always strive to improve your skills, but don't let self-doubt ruin your chances for success.

- Work on building and maintaining your self-confidence.

- Always remember that you have unique skills as a woman—skills that can greatly benefit your company.

- There is no one style of effective leadership. Be true to your natural abilities and develop your own style. Don't feel you need to mimic the male model.

- Women are just as capable as men of demonstrating the important qualities of a leader: intelligence, vision, integrity, good decision-making, etc. Be confident in your abilities.

- When searching for a job, look for companies that promote diversity in their leadership's demeanor and style.

- Develop a style of management wherein you are comfortable demonstrating leadership, while still feeling feminine.

- Don't let others' views shape your idea of what it means to be a powerful woman.

- Do the inner work that is necessary to be a leader and develop confidence in your abilities. Visualize how you would feel and act as a powerful woman.
- Don't be afraid of power, especially if you want to bring about change in your company, your nation ... and the world.
- If you experience negative effects from menstruation or pregnancy, discuss the issue with your supervisor, and try to reach a beneficial solution for yourself and your company.
- Stand up for your deepest desires. Don't let anyone take them away from you.
- Know that women's time for business leadership has come; many women have unique skills that companies need to be successful. Be grateful that you're not one of the good old boys.

○ ○ ○ ○

CHAPTER 20
Women Are Destined to Excel

- Don't let a discriminatory action or remark negate all the progress that women have made. Temporary setbacks will occur.
- Let go of the injustices of the past, face your fears, and move into your power. Create the world you want for yourself and your daughters.
- Women's progress cannot be stopped. The bottom line will win out. Decide if you want to be part of the progress—and go for it! I wish you all success.

Questions to Consider

CHAPTER 1
Earning Entry into the Business World

1. What kind of degrees do you think are most valued by the business community?
2. Do your career aspirations match what you love to do and are good at?
3. How important is it to know whether you are analytical, intuitive, or both? How could such self-knowledge influence your career choices?
4. Have you developed a plan for how to achieve your career aspirations?
5. How can parents help their daughters achieve success in their careers?
6. Do you think recruitment firms still discriminate against women? If so, how can this be changed?
7. What would you do if you were asked to dress in a provocative manner for your job?
8. Do you think giving up on your dreams and desires could have serious effects on your emotional and physical well-being?

o o o o

CHAPTER 2
Blatant Discrimination

1. Has blatant discrimination been replaced by more subtle forms of discrimination? Can you identify ways in which women are still being discriminated against?
2. Can you identify any situations in which women are not welcomed or

made to feel as comfortable as men?
3. Have you ever seen another woman being discriminated against? If so, what did you do, and what do you wish you had done?
4. What would you do if you suspect or know that you are being paid unfairly?
5. Do you ever feel angry about how you are treated in the workforce? If so, what should you do about it?

○ ○ ○ ○

CHAPTER 3
Sexual Harassment

1. What do you consider to be forms of sexual harassment?
2. Is a flattering remark in terms of your physical appearance acceptable?
3. What would you do if you received or witnessed sexual comments, or were sexually harassed in other ways?
4. Do you think filing a sexual harassment complaint hurts a woman's chance for promotion?
5. How effective do you think the #MeToo movement has been?
6. Do you believe that some men resent women for taking their jobs? If so, how is their resentment demonstrated?

○ ○ ○ ○

CHAPTER 4
Intimidation

1. How prevalent do you think intimidation and bullying are in the workplace?
2. What forms of intimidation or bullying have you been a victim of or observed? How did you handle the situation, and would you handle it the same way again?

3. What would you do if you were given an unreasonable assignment, or insufficient time or resources to complete a job?
4. How do you feel about whistleblowers?
5. Are there circumstances when it is appropriate to be a whistleblower?

○ ○ ○ ○

CHAPTER 5

Responsibility Without the Title, Pay, or Promotion

1. Why are women promoted less frequently to higher positions than men?
2. Why do you think the wage gap for women still exists?
3. What would you do if you were given work that was above your title and pay?
4. What is the best way to ask for a promotion or salary increase?
5. Do you think the phrase "power corrupts" is true? If so, how does one avoid being corrupted?

○ ○ ○ ○

CHAPTER 6

Support and Lack of Support (or Worse)

1. Do men support women in the workforce more than women support each other?
2. How important is it for women to support each other?
3. Do you think women support each other in the same way that men support each other?
4. What do you think about women showing emotion at work or crying?
5. What kind of experience should CEO candidates possess?
6. Do you think it is important to have both staff and line operational

experience to become a CEO?

7. If a woman chooses to marry, how important is it to have a supportive spouse?

8. What kind of family-oriented support programs are most important to you?

9. What are your views on women setting clear priorities about family versus career?

∘ ∘ ∘ ∘

CHAPTER 7

A Choice: Act Tough or Be Viewed as Weak

1. Do you know women who act tough, cold, or harsh at work? What is your reaction to them?

2. Do you think it is important for women to emulate the behavior of successful businessmen? What do you think is the ideal demeanor for a female executive?

3. Are there female workers whose style you admire?

4. How would you react to a woman who demands equal status and pay?

5. What would you do if you witnessed someone being humiliated?

6. What makes a woman strong or appear to be strong?

∘ ∘ ∘ ∘

CHAPTER 8

Using Sex Appeal in the Workplace

1. How do you feel about the use of sexuality to influence business decisions?

2. What would you do if you were a supervisor and saw one of your female employees flirting in some way to gain support?

3. Should women try to look as attractive as possible in the workplace?

4. What is the ideal dress for a businesswoman?
5. How does physical appearance affect a woman's confidence? Should it?
6. What are your views regarding affairs in the workplace?

○ ○ ○ ○

CHAPTER 9
The Unique Challenge of Meetings

1. What would you do if you were in a meeting and witnessed another woman being ignored? What would you do if you were ignored?
2. Do you think men tend to support other men more than they support women in meetings?
3. Do you think females or other minorities tend to support each other more than they do others?
4. Have you observed the communication style of a woman as being either helpful or hurtful to her career?
5. How should women speak in meetings in order to have their comments be heard and acknowledged?

○ ○ ○ ○

CHAPTER 10
Recognition

1. Do you think women are adequately recognized for their accomplishments? If not, why do you think this is so?
2. Do you think the good-old-boys' club mentality is still prevalent in corporate America?
3. How do you think women compare to men in terms of leadership skills?
4. Why do you think women lead only 8% of Fortune 500 companies in the U.S.?

CHAPTER 11
Smacking Up Against the Glass Ceiling

1. How do you define strength and weakness as it applies to both men and women in the workplace?
2. Have you experienced a situation that has hurt you deeply in the workplace? Have you been unable to forgive and move on?
3. Should women act "tough" in order to avoid being seen as weak?
4. What does it mean to be a strong, powerful woman?
5. What would you do if you hit the glass ceiling in a company?
6. What would you do if you were overlooked for a position for which you are qualified?

○ ○ ○ ○

CHAPTER 12
Compensation Disparity

1. Why do you think inequity in pay still exists?
2. How important is salary compensation to you? Are there things such as work flexibility that are more important to you?
3. What should you do if you find out you are paid less than a man for doing the same or similar job?
4. When will women gain equal pay?

○ ○ ○ ○

CHAPTER 13
The New Millennium—Still Second-in-Command

1. Do you think men possess a natural ability to exude more confidence and presence than women? Is this a learned capability?
2. How do women overcome decades of negative feelings about discrimination?

3. How do you think the U.S. compares to other countries in terms of female leadership?

○ ○ ○ ○

CHAPTER 14
Understanding Negative Perceptions

1. Do you shirk from getting negative feedback from bosses or colleagues, or do you ask for criticism in order to improve your performance?
2. How comfortable are you working in a predominantly male environment? What are some things you can do to increase your comfort level?
3. Do you think your skills and background vary substantially from most men's?
4. Do you think it is important that your interests be similar to those of your male colleagues?
5. How much are you willing to change to fit into the good-old-boys' club?

○ ○ ○ ○

CHAPTER 15
Losing a Job

1. Do you think a higher percentage of women are fired than men?
2. Do you think EEOC laws have been effective in protecting women's rights?
3. How should someone handle serious conflict with a boss?
4. If you were fired, or if your position was eliminated in some way that you believed to be unjust, would you sign a contract releasing the company from all wrongdoing, or would you attempt to take legal action against the company?

CHAPTER 16
Becoming CEO

1. What is the best path to becoming CEO?
2. What role does luck or chance play in advancement?
3. What are your thoughts about male-dominated organizations in business and politics?
4. Would you like to see more women hold CEO and other top-level positions? If so, why?
5. If you attained a top-level position in a major corporation, do you see yourself using your power and authority differently than past leaders?

∘ ∘ ∘ ∘

CHAPTER 17
Looking Back

1. Do you focus on the positives or negatives about your current job, i.e., do you see your glass as half empty or half full?
2. How do you handle failures? Do you think they can make a positive difference in your life?
3. Do you take time to evaluate how satisfied or dissatisfied you are in your job?
4. Do you take time to be grateful for your job, or are you only focused on the next opportunity?

∘ ∘ ∘ ∘

CHAPTER 18
Discrimination Still Exists

1. Do you think that women will continue to face discrimination in the workplace?
2. Do you know women who have been able to successfully manage a senior-level career and a family? What are some of the keys to their success?

3. If discrimination against women continues, do you think it is because men don't want to give up power? Are there other reasons?

○ ○ ○ ○

CHAPTER 19
Yourself: The Final Barrier

1. Are you aware of gender or racial prejudices that you have developed based on past experiences in your life?

2. Do you believe a woman can be as competent as a man in performing top jobs, e.g., President of the United States?

3. How much importance do you place on education and experience?

4. Do you agree that the core qualities of intelligence, vision, objectivity, integrity, along with good communication skills and the ability to lead are the necessary qualities for the leaders of tomorrow? Are there other qualities that you think are important? How do leaders of today reflect these qualities?

5. How should women act in business so they are not perceived as being indecisive, weak, or ineffectual?

6. Are you afraid of being viewed as powerful?

7. Do you think your chance of attracting and keeping a spouse or partner is less likely if you are viewed as successful and powerful?

8. Do you think powerful women who have achieved position and authority are viewed as being less feminine? If so, how can they resolve this conflict within themselves?

9. How can a woman learn to listen to her own voice and trust herself?

10. What are your deepest desires? How will you achieve them?

11. Are you comfortable owning and telling others about your accomplishments?

12. Why is equality important?

CHAPTER 20
Women Are Destined to Excel

1. Do you believe that the time has come for women to be the predominant leaders of business? If so, why?

2. Do you think equality for women and minorities will be attained in your lifetime?

3. What can companies do to help women in the workforce become successful, especially after the toll that the Covid-19 pandemic has taken on women?

4. Do you believe women will do a better job at leadership than men have done in the past? If so, in what way?

5. Can—and should—women help men feel comfortable with female leadership? If so, how?

References

1. Quantifying America's Gender Wage Gap by Race/Ethnicity, *National Partnership for Women & Families, Fact Sheet*, Januray 2022. https://www.nationalpartnership.org/our-work/resources/economic-justice/fair-pay/americas-women-and-the-wage-gap.pdf

2. Chip Cutter, "The Pandemic's Toll on Women's Careers," *The Wall Street Journal*, September 27, 2021, (R6).

3. Emma Hinchliffe, "The female CEOs on this year's Fortune 500 just broke three all-time records," *Fortune*, June 2, 2021, https://fortune.com/2021/06/02/female-ceos-fortune-500-2021.

4. See endnotes 34-37 for studies.

5. Richard N. Bowles, *What Color Is Your Parachute?: A Practical Manual for Job-Hunters and Career-Changers* (Ten Speed Press, Crown Publishing Group: New York, 2017).

6. Sheryl Sandberg, "Women Are Leaning In—But They Face Pushback," *The Wall Street Journal*, September 27, 2016 (R2). Rachel Thomas, president of Lean In, contributed to the essay.

7. http://legal-dictionary.thefreedictionary.com/sexual+harrassment.

8. https://www.ncbi.nlm.nih.gov/pmc/articles/PMC6127768/
https://www.nytimes.com/2018/12/10/health/mind-epigenetics-genes.html

9. Susannah Wellford, "Cultivating the Old Girls Club," *U.S. News*, https://www.usnews.com/topics/articles/2016-8-29.

10. Rachel Emma Silverman, "High Finance and Family-Friendly? KKR Is Trying," *The Wall Street Journal* September 27, 2016 (R6).

11. Cara Christ, "Desktops and Diapers," *The Arizona Republic*, March 11, 2017 (16A).

12. Dana Mattioli, "Programs to Promote Female Manager Win Citations," *The Wall Street Journal*, January 30, 2007 (B7).

13. Chip Cutter, "The Pandemic's Toll on Women's Careers," *The Wall Street Journal*, September 27, 2021, (R6).

14. Vanessa Fuhrmans and Lauren Weber, "Redefining Ambition," *The Wall Street Journal*, September 27, 2021, (R1, R4-5); Source Gusto.

15. Joann S. Lublin, "At Some Firms, A Push to Bring Mothers Back," *The Wall Street Journal*, September 27, 2021 (R2).

16. Alison Bowe, "Work-balance guidance for high-powered women," *The Chicago Tribune*, July 23, 2017 (Section 6, 5).

17 Rachel Feinzeig, "On Negotiating," *The Wall Street Journal*, September 27, 2016 (R7).

18 Georgia Wells, Jeff Horwitz, and Deepa Seetharaman, "Facebook Knows Instagram Is Toxic For Teen Girls, Its Research Shows, *The Wall Street Journal*, September 15, 2021

19 Sarah Dreher, "The Average Woman Loses $407,760 Because of the Gender Wage Gap Over Her Lifetime," *Newsweek*, March 31, 2020 at https://www.newsweek.com.

20 Kelsy Gee, "Workarounds: How Gender Affects Funding For Women," *The Wall Street Journal*, July 12, 2017 (B10).

21 J.J. McCorvey and Julia Carpenter, "There's Another Gender Pay Gap: Stock Options," *The Wall Street Journal*, September 27, 2021 (R7); Sources: National Opinion research Center at the University of Chicago; Rutgers Institute for the Study of Employee Ownership and Profit Sharing.

22 Sandy Smith, "Workplace Bullying: How to Deal with Intimidation or Harassment," March 29, 2013 http://ehstoday.com/safety/workplace.

23 Karen Gifford, "Telling Women to Be Like Men Doesn't Work," February 12, 2014 at http://www.huffingtonpost.com/karen-gifford.

24 Rachel Feintzeig, "How to be Heard," with comments by Susan Hertzberg, former CEO of Boston Heart Diagnostics Corp, *The Wall Street Journal*, September 27, 2016 (R4).

25 Nikki Waller, "How Men and Women See the Workplace Differently," *The Wall Street Journal*, September 27, 2016 (R1).

26 *The Wall Street Journal*, September 30, 2020 (R1-9)

27 Douglas Belkin, "'I Just Feel Lost.' Young Men Abandon College," *The Wall Street Journal*, September 7, 2021 (A1, A9).

28 Richard Vedder and Braden Colegrove, "Why Men Are Disappearing on Campus," *The Wall Street Journal*, September 20, 2021, (A17).

29 Jennifer Palmieri, *She Proclaims: Our Declaration of Independence from a Man's World* (Grand Central Publishing, July 2020).

30 Arianna Huffington, "My Journey to the Top," *Newsweek*, October 15, 2007, 49.

31 Lauren Weber, "Women Trim Ambitions for Marriage, Study Says," *The Wall Street Journal*, January 25, 2017 (B6), with comments by Amanda Pallais, Leonardo Burstzyn, and Thomas Fujiwara.

32 Marianne Williamson, *A Return to Love* (HarperCollins Publishers, Inc., New York: 1992.)

33 Glennon Doyle Melton, "We're Not Fine, and We Do Care," *The Oprah Magazine*, July 2017, 31-32.

34 Joann S. Lublin, "The More Women in Power, The More Women in Power," *The Wall Street Journal*, September 27, 2016 (R4).

35 John Simons, "Women CEOs Bolster Sales, Report Says," *The Wall Street Journal*, December 14, 2016 (B5).

36 Rick Wartzman and Kelly Tang, "The High Price if Women Drop Out of Labor Force," *The Wall Street Journal*, October 26, 2020 (R14).

37 Alyssa Newcomb, https://www.nbcnews.com/business; December 30, 2020.

38 Lauren Weber, "Women Gain as Skills Shift for High-Paying Jobs," *The Wall Street Journal*, March 22, 2017 (B5).

39 Joann S. Lublin, "Rankings Defy Usual Gender Gap," *The Wall Street Journal*, June 1, 2017 (B2).

40 Brody Mullins, "Key Business Group Names Woman CEO For the First Time," *The Wall Street Journal*, February 10, 2021 (A5).

41 Laurence Norman, "WTO Appoints Nigerian as First Female Leader," *The Wall Street Journal*, February 16, 2021, (A9).

About the Author

DONNA FRIDRYCH was one of the first women consultants in the field of computer technology. Starting as a computer programmer, she climbed the corporate ladder to act as Chief Information Officer for United Airlines and later became CEO of the United Airlines Employees' Credit Union. As a marketing director, she traveled around the world conducting business in many foreign countries and relished the opportunity to get to know people from different cultures. As an entrepreneur, she owned an antiques business in a four-story Victorian house for many years and also co-owned a day spa. True to the "Renaissance Woman" label given to her by friends, she began her latest career as an author after retiring from the corporate world.

Donna currently spends winters in Arizona and summers at her lake home in northern Illinois with her long-term partner William and their two dogs, Valentino (Tino)—who got his name when he was rescued on Valentine's Day—and Natasha (Tasha), his adorable playmate.

Other books
by Donna Fridrych

WOMEN MUST SAVE THE WORLD!
A CALL TO ACTION

THE YEAR OF THE BUTTERFLY

www.ingramcontent.com/pod-product-compliance
Lightning Source LLC
Chambersburg PA
CBHW051943290426
44110CB00015B/2089